Joaquin Miller

The Building of the City Beautiful

Joaquin Miller

The Building of the City Beautiful

ISBN/EAN: 9783744790376

Printed in Europe, USA, Canada, Australia, Japan

Cover: Foto ©ninafisch / pixelio.de

More available books at **www.hansebooks.com**

THE BUILDING
OF
THE CITY BEAUTIFUL

By JOAQUIN MILLER

CAMBRIDGE & CHICAGO
PUBLISHED BY STONE &
KIMBALL IN THE YEAR
MDCCCXCIII

CONTENTS.

		PAGE
I.	An Old Woman with a Load of Wood	1
II.	"Feed my Sheep"	12
III.	"The Time is fulfilled, and the Kingdom of God is at Hand"	21
IV.	The Growing of a Soul	30
V.	How Beautiful!	37
VI.	The Sermon on the Mount	42
VII.	In the Sweat of thy Face	48
VIII.	The Christ in Egypt	52
IX.	Awaiting the Resurrection at Karnak	56
X.	The Voice of Toil	66
XI.	The Foundation Stones	73
XII.	The First Law of God	85
XIII.	Fallen by the Way	94
XIV.	Under the Olive-Trees	102
XV.	As when the Christ shall come again	114
XVI.		120

XVII.	IN HER PRESENCE AT LAST	127
XVIII.	GIVE US THIS DAY OUR DAILY BREAD	141
✓ XIX.	THE TOIL OF GOD	153
XX.	WHEN MAN IS NOT WATCHING MAN	162
XXI.		167
XXII.	THE TRULY BRAVE	173
XXIII.	GOING	182
XXIV.	PUT UP THY SWORD	187

THE BUILDING OF THE CITY BEAUTIFUL.

I. — AN OLD WOMAN WITH A LOAD OF WOOD.

" Now he is dead. Far hence he lies
In that lorn Syrian town ;
And o'er his grave with pitying eyes
The Syrian stars look down."

" How hardly shall they that have riches enter the kingdom of God. It is easier for a camel to go through the eye of a needle than for a rich man to enter the kingdom of God."

SIR MOSES MONTIFIORE, of the house of Rothschilds, and one of the very rich men in all the world, was in Jerusalem. It was his last of more than a score of pilgrimages to the Holy City.

He had founded little colonies near Bethlehem and in many places round about Jerusalem. True, he was very old now; but this remarkable man, who lived for more than a century, was still full of purpose.

His last coming had created quite a sensation among the Jews as a matter of course. The great hospital hard by, the burial-ground, the synagogue,—all these were his gifts to the Jewish people, and they were not ungrateful.

As for the Christians, they were scarcely less eager to see the very rich old man. Bibles were opened, and the lines at the head of this chapter were read over and over again.

The man's great age now compelled him to leave the direction of his work almost entirely to others. Still he must know all that had been done in his long absence in London. He wanted to know just how the little colonies were getting on. Were the people from Poland content? Were the peasant Jews from Russia united and tolerant of their less stalwart brothers? Strange how much stronger were those of the extreme North than those who had been for generations in Jerusalem and other warm lands!

There were Jews returning to Jerusalem from the banks of the Volga after an absence of a thousand years! and these were strong men. They had crept out from under the snows of Russia and come down to the city of David with hair almost yellow and eyes as blue as their sacred Syrian skies. Their expulsion from Jerusalem had surely done them good.

The Jews of all kinds and of all countries who had been established in their new homes by Sir Moses came pouring in through the various gates and passes on this day of his arrival.

And a little crowd of Christians, after reading over and over again the words of Christ to the ruler who was very rich, went down to a narrow pass leading to the dirty and dismal market in the valley of Jehoshaphat.

Peasants were crowding through the narrow pass, about which so much has been said and written, and about which really nothing, so far as the words of Christ are concerned, is known. And a tall, dark woman stood there, looking at the crowding peasants, — a young and strangely beautiful woman, silent, serene, dignified, and commanding.

Some of the people had heavy loads on their backs; one had a lamb, one carried only a dove. They were all on their way to market. They then would go and see Sir Moses, and possibly be able to beg some money.

How they did jostle and wrangle, and

abuse and bully one another! The man with only a dove to carry would not give an inch of road or room to an old woman who was bowed almost to the ground under a load of sticks.

It was altogether a sad picture, and the serenely beautiful face of the silent woman, who stood there on the edge of the group of garrulous tourists, grew sad at the sight of it.

Time, then, taught nothing. Each was for himself as of old. No pity, no sympathy, no sincerity! They were all mad, in haste to have done with their marketing so that they might run to where Sir Moses lodged and be the first to beg a little money.

But this tall, dark woman on the outside of the group of Christians was very patient. The dust of travel was still on her sable garments. She was seeking in vain for some gentle soul in that multitude of loud, aggressive, and half-savage Jews.

After the peasants had all crowded through and left the "Needle's Eye" to the inspection of the group of Christians, she turned with a sigh to go away.

Suddenly some one in the knot of people who held red guide-books in their hands, said emphatically and right in her face:

"That settles it for the rich man, I guess. Sir Moses ought to put his money on a camel's back and see if it could get through the Eye of the Needle, eh?"

There is an intoxication not always of the wine glass. Men and women say things and do things in foreign places, especially when in crowds, which they would not say and do if alone and at home. Set a guard at the portals; and if you cannot keep sober, you can at least keep silent. Every one at certain times and in certain places is entitled to his own thoughts. They are his property more entirely than his own money is his. He has journeyed far to meditate here. This rare moment has cost him much. And yet he oftentimes hears only a rushing of feet over sacred ground, and a Babel of voices in solemn abbey and sublime cathedral. At such times one thanks God that man is so very insignificant that he may not be heard far.

The tall, dark lady did not reply. She preferred to pass on and seem not to hear. The better portion of the crowd of tourists were angered; but as two or three laughed their assent the man repeated his remark to the silent woman, thinking, perhaps, that she did not understand English.

This young woman — was she a Jewess? — was travelling with Sir Moses Montifiore, as secretary, or something of the sort. The remarkable philanthropist, as said before, was making the last of more than a score of pilgrimages to the city of David. He had spent millions on millions in his noble effort to re-people Palestine.

As you go up toward Jerusalem from the sea you pass by pleasant little settlements, new and fair and verdant as if in Idaho. Indeed, nearly all of the land of Syria seems much like the varied plains that stretch from the slopes of Idaho southward to the sea of Cortez, — cattle and sheep and horses, little fields of grain, orchards, thrift and industry, in spots, as on our plains to-day.

It was mainly to look after these, and to add to them with those of his people who were being driven out of Russia, that the old Israelite had resolved to come once more all the way from London at his advanced age.

And it was the good fortune of his coming that caused a new man of the new world and this wondrously beautiful and strong and strange woman of the old world to meet together at the Eye of the Needle. Let us not recount the details of their meeting. Strong souls meet suddenly, as rivers meet when rushing to the same great sea.

"Yes, that gate settles the fate of the rich man," added one of the crowd. The new man of the new world was indignant.

And now her great, dark eyes took fire. Her brow grew dark. Her dark immensity of hair seemed to take on a faint tinge of fire about the face and at the tips. The new man of the new world did not know at this time, nor did she deign to tell any one, — for she was a woman of few words, like all really great women, — that she stood in very close relation to one of the very richest men in the world.

Again she turned to go in silence. The man, who had only half concealed his indignation at the persistence of the garrulous tourist, stepped forward, hat in hand, but said nothing. He was not of the group of people who had come, guide-books in hand, to see the so-called Eye of the Needle. Perhaps he had seen all there was to see there long before. You can generally distinguish travelled from untravelled people by their quiet bearing.

The woman turned the third time to pass in silence; but still she persisted in glancing back.

Is it the remnant of wild beast in us still that makes all hunted or wounded human beings turn quickly about to give battle? But here was a battle in her own heart. She was bursting with indignation, yet she had trained her soul to soar above resentment. So the cloud that lowered about her glorious face blew over as the stranger stood respectfully before her. But she did not address herself to him or seem to note him at all. She was concerned only to answer the man who had so persistently referred to the fate of the rich man. Slowly and softly she said: —

"Yes, I have read, and I have also heard it from the pulpit, that it was to this gate that Jesus Christ referred when he spoke of the rich man."

The tall, grand woman drew her loose mantle more closely about her throat, and lifting her eyes looked away toward the hill on which stood the camp of Titus when Jerusalem was overthrown; and without intending it, or really knowing that she did so, she looked entirely above the man before her as she went on in an earnest, far-away voice: —

"Yes, men have published, and men have stood up and proclaimed, that Jesus referred to this gate when he spoke of the eye of the needle, because it was so extremely hard for a camel to pass through here. That is to say, a camel could pass through it only with great difficulty." She paused, her proud lip curled as she continued:—

"How pitiful and helpless this interpretation, and yet how simple and sublime the few plain words of Jesus Christ! Let us read them!" and as if reading in the air she repeated: "How hardly shall they that have riches enter into the kingdom of God. It is easier for a camel to go through the eye of a needle than for a rich man to enter the kingdom of God."

She paused, still looking far away; then she said: "That is to say, it is literally easier for a camel to pass through the eye of a needle than for a man to pass into heaven after death with his riches on his back. He must lay aside his wealth at the door of death, and enter the kingdom of God poor as the poorest."

She turned to go, and then again came back.

"Sir Moses Montifiore," she said gently, "is a very rich man to-day, one of the richest in the world; yet surely if any rich man enters, or ever has entered, the kingdom of God he will. No, no! To say that the divine young Jew, Jesus, shut the gates of heaven in the face of a man because he had riches on earth, would be to say that he was not Christ at all. True, he said to the rich man, a ruler who came to ask him the way, 'Sell all that thou hast and distribute unto the poor, and come and follow me.' But this must have meant a literal following; for soon he took unto him the twelve and said unto them, 'Behold, we go up to Jerusalem, and all things that are written by the prophets concerning the Son of Man shall be accomplished.'"

The crowd had melted away, all but one man. This man had bowed his head as she continued to speak. When she ceased, his chin was on his breast and his hat was still in his hand. He knew he was hearing the voice of a soul. But who could she be? She spoke English fluently, yet with an accent. She had been conversing in French with a party as he approached. There was a Catholic priest in this French party, and was she not a Jewess? A Jewess knowing more of Christ than Christians!

"All civilized peoples, whether Jews or Christians, of to-day are comparatively rich; and when this world shall be all civilized we shall all be very rich. Yet shall we not all enter the kingdom of God?"

These few last words of the dark and silent woman were said as if entirely to herself.

II. — "FEED MY SHEEP."

Come, let us ponder; it is fit —
  Born of the poor, born to the poor —
The poor of purse, the poor of wit
  Were first to find God's opening door,
Were first to climb the ladder, round by round,
That fell from heaven's door unto the ground.

God's poor came first, the very first!
  God's poor were first to see, to hear,
To feel the light of heaven burst
  Full on their faces far or near,
His poor were first to follow, first to fall!
What if at last His poor stand first of all?

THIS is not entirely a love story. It is not a religious or irreligious story. It is the record of one, or rather two persons who believed that man is not only entitled to the pursuit of happiness but to the attainment of happiness, real and substantial, upon earth.

The woman, Miriam, was indeed a Jewess, a Jewess — and it is said with reverence — as Mary, the mother of Christ, was a Jewess.

She was from Russia, or, more properly, from Siberia, where she had spent her hard, bitter girlhood sitting by her broken and exiled father's bed. Death, his death, had liberated them both at once, and she had gone direct to London and found employment with Sir Moses in his effort to ameliorate the condition of his people.

Her trustworthiness, her quiet wisdom in all matters intrusted to her, had soon placed her in the highest position and most influential relations with the great men of her race. But she was growing, growing rapidly, and soon she grew beyond the narrow limits of race or creed. She came to believe in all good of all religions. Forms and fashions she put aside, as the cloth that covered His face was put aside on the third day.

Miriam was a devout worshipper in the synagogue. She had knelt quite as devoutly before the Greek cross in the Kremlin, had bowed low in the mosque of Omar, and had crossed herself reverently in St. Peter's; for she loved all peoples, and she pitied all peoples in all their pitiful forms of idolatry.

Her heart was almost broken here, this first morning of her arrival at the city of David and Solomon. For here, in the very dust and ashes of the Temple, she saw the same old hates, enmities, jealousies, narrowness, and uncleanliness of soul and of body;

narrow and unclean as the little gate through which her people crowded.

What had two thousand years done for God's people? They had not been borne forward at all. The world, Pagan, Christian, Jew, under the old system of selfish money-getting, place and power seeking, was still the same. The old order of things had been on trial, in all climes and under all conditions, for years and years, and what was the result? Sorrow, suicide, despair. Man stood staring on before him, even in the most civilized places and under the most favorable conditions, and kept asking, asking, " Is life worth living?"

"God in heaven!" she cried; "with all this glory of sky and earth, the sweet air, the flowers and birds, our boundless capacity for enjoyment, shall the world still be joyless? Why, every breath, even to the most wretched, should be to him as a benediction. Yes," she continued very seriously, "this old order of things has been on trial long enough; and if we could and should restore Jerusalem to-day in all her ancient splendor, what then? Why, some new Rome would rise to encompass her. There would be born within her walls another Simon and another John, with all their burning hates and jealousies; and the streets would run with blood the same as two thousand years ago. Then why restore her? Men would stand on the Temple's porch, as in the high places of London and Paris to-day, and gravely ask, 'Is life worth living?'"

The man, with his hat in his hand and his head bowed, was again before her. He lifted his face slowly to hers.

"You were pained at what those tourists said?"

"Those tourists? I had forgotten them. But I was greatly pained to see these poor people with their burthens, great or small, crowding in such rude competition to the market."

"'Competition is the life of trade,'" he said lightly; not that he felt that there was any truth or any good of any sort in this old saw, but he said it as all of us who have not considered the sanctity of speech will say silly things. Ah, how much wiser we should all be were we dumb as beasts, or, at least, as silent!

In a moment the flashing of her dark eyes told him he had not said quite what he should have said.

"'Competition the life of trade!'" she

began, as if to herself. "These old sayings are more than millstones about the neck of this world. Trade! what is trade? No wonder that the English gentlemen centuries ago forbade those in trade to sit at their tables or to come into the presence of their king. Not one of the million tradesmen ever grew one grain of corn, or fed so much as one little bird. They battle to the death among themselves in this competition of trade; ninety in every hundred fall on this field of competition; they sacrifice time, truth, honor, energy, life itself, in competition for the robbery of the people. This very competition makes them hard, heartless to one another. They should, in very defence of themselves, be forbidden this fatal competition, destroying their souls and their bodies together."

The man caught in his breath. He raised his two hands, came up and threw both out to her heartily. She did not misunderstand. She grasped his two hands as earnestly as he extended them. The world is round, and he came into her life as a stately ship enters a harbor after circling the earth.

Who was he? It hardly matters. The future of our story and of this man is not behind us. Enough to say that he had been born near the banks of a great river in the far-away new world, nearly half a century before. And this meant that he had met and walked with poverty and woe in the wilderness.

Faint and dubious was the light that fell across the path of any one born of his period and station there. Gentleness was not encouraged. Man grappled with man and contended from the time when he left the cradle till he reached the grave. Cabin homes under the beech and maple trees, that ought to have been Edens, were often homes of enmity, bitterness, and continual unhappiness. Neighbor was often arrayed against neighbor. Bitter family feuds grew out of the most trivial of matters, and the nearest neighbors were often the bitterest enemies. True, they would meet now and then at the little church, but would scarcely speak one to another. They would meet sometimes in the graveyard, drop tears in the grave together, as they covered up their dead, and then go away. Let the truth be told. Let romance picture no road of roses here. All men were unhappy, miserably unhappy here. Their feuds often ended in battles to the death, as in Kentucky to this day.

And was this the fault of the good God?

Not so. Plenty there was, abundance after its kind, for all. Wild game, wild fruits, wild nuts, and in abundance, and to be had for the taking! and yet man oftentimes went hunting for man as for a wild beast. This wretched hatred of man toward man, this continual unhappiness, was so conspicuous on every hand that this man, even in his childhood, had noted it.

When travel came with time, and carried him far and wide and up from the cabin door to the castle hall, all the way, and at all times, and under all circumstances and all conditions, he found his fellow-men continually unhappy. The king on his throne he found as full of rivalry and contention as the pioneer in his cabin.

And he found that all history, sacred and profane, rose up and testified, from King David down, that "all is vanity and vexation of spirit."

And he read that one mighty in power and opulence had cut upon a column of granite in the four corners of his kingdom, ages ago, this fearful confession: "Eat, drink, and love. The rest is not worth a fillip."

Travelling in Persia, our searcher for happy people had picked up a tradition which read thus: "Send forth, O King! search and find a happy man. Take that man's shirt and wear it, and thou, too, shalt be happy."

And the king sent forth men, and they searched, and they searched throughout the four corners of his kingdom. And in the third year, as they came down a pleasant mountain pass where water flowed by the mouth of a cave half hidden in laden vines, they saw a man playing joyously on his pipe.

"You seem happy!"

"Happy! I am happy. The sun is warm, the grapes are sweet, and God is good. Oh, yes, I am very, very happy."

"Then come, come with us. Your fortune is made, our fortunes are made! Come, rise up and go with us."

"And where shall I go, my good masters?"

"Why, go with us to the palace of the king, and the king will give you the fortune of a prince."

"And what shall I give the king in return for all this, my good masters?"

"Nothing, nothing at all except the shirt you wear."

"Ah, my good masters, I was never bothered with a shirt."

So saying, he threw aside the sheepskin that hung about his shoulders, and dropping his lips to his pipe, played pleasantly as the weary men on their weary camels rode wearily on in this hopeless search.

Yes, here was a happy man, but of what manner? He was not a man in the true sense of the word. He was more nearly a domestic and kindly beast. His negative happiness was surely not the sort of happiness to which man made in the image of God was destined.

Should a bestial king perpetuate to all posterity the outrageous declaration on his columns of granite and brass that there is nothing better in life than to "eat, drink, and be merry"?

Even were there a grain of truth in his folly, any man with a heart in him would be made miserable all the time when sober enough to reflect how many, or rather how few, how very, very few could, under such a condition of things, be allowed to "eat, drink, and love."

What wonder, then, that this stranger threw out his two hands to this brave and beautiful woman who stood there on the ruins of Solomon's Temple, lamenting the enmities and hates and common misery of the human race!

III. — "THE TIME IS FULFILLED, AND THE KINGDOM OF GOD IS AT HAND."

UNDER THE SYRIAN STARS.

Dear Bethlehem, the proud repose
  Of conscious worthiness is thine.
Rest on. The Arab comes and goes,
  But farthest Saxon holds thy shrine
More sacred in his stouter Christian hold
Than England's heaped-up iron house of gold.

Thy stony hill is heaven's stair;
  Thine every stone some storied gem.
Oh, thou art fair and very fair,
  Thou holy, holy Bethlehem!
Thy very dust more dear than dust of gold
Against my glorious sunset waters rolled.

And here did glean the lowly Ruth;
  Here strode her grandson, fierce and fair,
Strode forth in all his kingly youth
  And tore the ravening she-bear.
Here Rachel sleeps. Here David, thirsting, cried
For just one drop from yonder trickling tide.

ONE night this man and woman walked together in the Garden of Gethsemane under the Syrian stars, and she said, in the same sad, far-away voice: —

" That strong man who carried the dove should have carried the old woman's wood.

She should have remained at home, or, if she desired, should have been carried in a cart, sitting on her burthen and resting from the gathering of it, looking about her at the flowers and the birds, or above her at these wondrously beautiful blue skies of Syria."

"That is a great truth," he cried; "and I would joy in being a missionary in the cause of that truth; but what are we to do when every man, from the throne down, must have his own selfish way, except when forced to submit?"

He leaned his head to hear what she might say. Possibly her thought was in line with his own plan for the redemption of man from man. As they passed on under an ancient olive tree she began slowly: —

"Let us be very practical. The salvation of the world now depends on a little hard, sound sense only. It has been going around and around and around, like a little whirling, merry-go-round with helpless and heedless children, till its head has grown dizzy. We have costly churches here and costly cathedrals there, of every nation and of every name; enough to buy horses, ploughs, carriages, — all things needed for all who need them. We claim to build those temples for the people; yet the people are broken in body and in spirit. Some of them will sleep in the streets and alleys to-night, while every church and temple stands empty and bolted against God's poor. The rich must have a place where they can come and find God now and then; and so God's houses are all bolted and barred, while God's poor sleep in the rain and frost before the bolted doors."

The man looked away from the Mount of Olives. He began to wonder whether the great, big world, after its cruel fashion, would be pleased to brand this woman as a nihilist, or a communist. Finally he said:—

"Surely we are in the wilderness; but is there any way out?"

"There is a column of cloud by day and a pillar of fire by night. Look back, back even beyond Exodus, back to the first cry and confession of sin from man to his Maker. 'The woman tempted me and I did eat.' And she — the serpent tempted her. And behold! when your Christ prayed he prayed this one prayer, after the prayer for bread and for forgiveness: 'Lead us not into temptation!'"

"I see, I see," he said; " it is plain indeed. You would not have the man tempted to crowd past the old woman with the load on her back in his haste to be first at the market. You would not let the poor, bent body be tempted to give the price of her load to sustain her broken body. You would not open the houses of dissipation to the poor at night, and at the same time lock the doors of God's house."

The woman's face took on a new and glorious light.

"Man is good," she began; "man is almost entirely good. Yet if he was tempted to be bad in Eden where all was so perfect and lovely, how shall we dare hope he will not fall in the terrible trials with which he is so continually beset to-day?"

"There seems to me but one thing to do: Pray the prayer and live the prayer of Jesus Christ, 'Lead us not into temptation,'" said the man earnestly and with bowed head.

"Ay, then," said the woman at his side, "then we shall see the cloud of smoke by day, after we have followed the pillar of fire in the darkness; and we can then read, and can then comprehend these other words of Jesus Christ: 'The time is fulfilled, and the kingdom of God is at hand.'"

"Yes, yes," he murmured to himself; and yet he feared that all this would melt and fade away, as had melted and faded out of sight so many theories and pretty sermons to which he had listened for years. It all seemed too bright and beautiful to be true. But that plan of hers to buy a cart for the old woman to ride in, on her load of wood, was not the plan of a theorist. Let many churches be sold, since they are so rarely in use, and then many old women with bent backs could have carts to ride in. Carry the idea on and on and on; and then no one could jostle any one at all. The temptation to jostle an old woman with a load of wood on her back would be removed.

"Let this idea enter all departments of life. Let it be possible for all to ride. Let every man be a king, and there will be no contention for thrones," urged the woman, earnestly, as she saw that her listener was intensely interested. "Listen to me. God is the great emancipator of man; not Lincoln, not the Czar. God has written the emancipation proclamation of man in lightning on the walls of heaven. A message that consumed half a year a little time ago is now delivered in an hour. A single hand on an engine will give out in a day garments that cost a thousand hands a year to fashion half a century back. And so with bread, with houses, with all things. God has emancipated man, I say, but man still enthralls man."

They had slowly descended, and walked toward the city. It is all plain, this which we offer you here. The way by which we set out to lead up out of Egypt may appear to you a desert course; it may seem tortuous, may look to you like the contortions of a serpent, of the brazen serpent for the fainting people to look upon; but bear in mind we, the human race, are in the wilderness. Faith must be put to the test, and it may be forty years before we look down into the promised land. It may be that none of us shall live to enter there. But that makes the exodus none the less a religious duty. You and you and you may turn back to the flesh-pots of Egypt; the writer may perish in the wilderness and no man know his burial-place; but that shall make the truth none the less truth as the centuries roll forward.

As they stood in the serene starlight before the low white door of the little hotel, the woman reached the man her hand to say good-by and let him go his way; then she said slowly:—

"The kingdom of heaven is at hand when temptation is not at hand. And this is the whole story, as briefly as it can be stated. In this search for the highway of happiness for man I did not at once decide that all men are good at heart," she said. "In the course of my hard life I have found so many sad exceptions to this general rule that it seemed impossible to accept it. But that one piteous little sentence which is indeed the substance of the prayer of Jesus Christ, — 'Lead us not into temptation,' — seemed so full of confession that the conviction gradually fastened itself upon me that all men are at least trying to be good. If the prayer had read, 'Make us strong against temptation;' if the prayer had said, 'Be with us in the hour of temptation' — but the confession, 'Lead us not into temptation, or we shall surely fall,' includes all men and all that is in man. A penny may be a temptation to one, a kingdom to another; and so 'Lead us not into temptation.' Stop and consider a moment how unequal are all men and how unequal are our human laws. Some of us are strong, so strong that ordinary things are not temptations; but a poor wretch bearing a load of sticks on her back comes by, is weary, tempted to drink, and falls. And we who are above the little thing that tempted her turn and take God's sunlight out of her eyes for days together. Better take temptation out of her way; for God made her, and she is good, whatever man may make her. Whoever she may be, she is God's, and she is sacred, wherever she may be."

Pausing a time, she lifted her face and said earnestly: "Read attentively the very first chapter of the Bible, — 'and God saw that it was good.' Time after time is this repeated: 'And God saw that it was good.' 'And God saw all that he had made, and behold, it was very good.' And yet man dares say by word and deed continually that it is not good. Why, even the wild beasts are good. The fiercest lion of the desert is bravely good."

For an instant, as she ceased to speak, her lifted face had all the awful splendor of a lioness aroused.

She suddenly again gave him her hand and went hastily in at the low, white door. He stood alone, looking after her for a long time, and then went his way, a truer man and a better man by a great deal than he had ever been before.

The stars were shining through his inmost soul; for he loved her so. Loved her! He deified her. Beautiful as was her face and form, her beauty of soul, her unselfish sincerity and devotion to the cause of humanity made her his angel, his ideal.

He had hated, or at least feared and avoided women up to the time when he met her. Now a woman was his whole world. She was his earth and his heaven. Where would it end?

IV. — THE GROWING OF A SOUL.

Hear ye this parable. A man
   Did plant a garden. Vine and tree
Alike, in course of time, began
   To put forth fair and pleasantly.
The rains of heaven, the persuading sun
Came down alike on each and every one.

Yet some trees wilful grew, and some
   Strong vines grew gayly in the sun,
With gaudy leaves, that ever come
   To naught. And yet, each flaunting one
Did flourish on triumphantly and glow
Like sunset clouds in all their moving show.

But lo ! the harvest found them not.
   The soul had perished from them. Mould
And muck and leaf lay there to rot,
   And furnish nourishment untold
To patient tree and lowly creeping vine
That grew as grew the Husbandman's design.

Hear then this lesson ; hear and heed ·
   I say that chaff shall perish ; say
Man's soul is like unto a seed
   To grow unto the Judgment Day.
It grows and grows if he will have it grow;
It perishes if he must have it so.

THIS man had seen the world, — all the civilized world, and more of the savage world also than many. For years he had travelled continually, travelled in a quiet way, keeping always among the poor and toiling. He wrote, taught, toiled with his hands, turned his hand to what he could, but all the time remained with his peers, the poor; not the low, mind you. Now and then he happened to write something that attracted the attention of the thinkers; and then some strong hands would reach out and lift him up into the great white light that beats upon thrones. But he was glad always to get down and out of it all, to get back to his peers, the poor; for there was work to do.

It had begun to appear to him as hardly fair that the man who laid the brick and mortar and made the great sewers through the mud and malaria of Paris and London and such like cities should not be able to eat meat more than twice each week without robbing his children, while the man who did no work at all, but walked about with his face held high in the sweet air, should have meat and wine twice each day; ay, many kinds of meat and wine if he so desired.

He said one day to one of these men down there in a deep sewer, as he leaned over and bade him look up: "Why do not you men unite and build a city of your own? Go to America, go away out in the unsettled deserts of Arizona or Mexico, find a warm, beautiful spot, plant vines, build a city, and have peace and plenty all your own."

The man shook his head slowly, and finally said, "No; we built Paris and we are going to burn Paris, and then have peace and plenty here."

This was a few months before the Commune.

Now the burning of Paris was not so much, — not so much in comparison with the deep and terrible hate in the heart of that man. Man can easily make a city, but it takes God to make a man. And it takes even God generations upon generations, under His own laws, to build up a single manly, sweet-souled human man out of such hardened and bitter material as that.

Here is what the woman whom he met in Jerusalem wrote to him, soon after they first met as described, on the subject of city building : —

"The flow of population is steadily to the great centres of the earth. This cannot be stopped or stayed. The people are pouring into the cities. The only thing to be done is to make the cities fit for their reception. There is not to-day one farm-house in all Russia or France. A new order of things has come upon cities and villages, and the man who loves his fellow-men must now meet this new order of things like a practical man.

"The man who lives for himself only lives for a very small man.

"Man should lay the foundation stones of his city where God has laid them. Why will he not choose the beautiful mountain slopes of America, instead of the marshes of Liverpool, the mud of London, or the malaria-reeking ruins of Rome? Is it because he has not hope, heart, unity, strength?

"Well, then, since these workers, these world-builders, have not these qualities, let those who love the world go forth, find sunny slopes and natural hills of health, and there, with God to help them, lay the corner-stones of the new cities under this new order of things, for these new people who so persistently and so helplessly pour into the cities.

"Man must be saved from man. Jesus Christ lived and died to save man; to save man from man, not man from God; to save man from himself by His example of patient pity and forgiveness and the precepts of the Sermon on the Mount.

"Is man an antediluvian monster, that he shall for all time wallow in the mud and mire of some old seaport? Is man a beast, that he should be led along forever with blinds before his eyes for fear that he may see the light and run away?

"Let us go forth and build a city where there are roomy, sunlit, untrod mountain-sides; build it on the beautiful foundation stones that God has laid with his own hand; and let us lay the moral and social foundations on the sacred and immortal precepts of the Sermon on the Mount; build in Faith and Hope and Charity, and leave the rest to time, to God's first-born.

"No, you should not compel man to believe that Christ died to save man from God. Let all believe as God has given them to believe, as to whether Christ died to save man from man or to save man from God. Nor should you insist that Christ is the only begotten Son of God. This has been argued by sword and pen, till every venerable city that was ever founded has been drenched in blood and tears. Only let each man try to believe in man and obey the precepts of the Sermon on the Mount. There are many sons of God.

The good God made us all very beautiful in soul and body to begin with; and very, very happy too; therefore we know that He desires us to be continually happy and continually beautiful. And if we are not continually happy and continually beautiful is it the fault of God or the fault of man?

"Indisputably it is entirely the fault of man. Let us then see that man be made less miserable. Let us look less dogmatically after God, who can well afford to pity us for our wrongs to His beautiful image. And now let us go forth with the Sermon on the Mount in hand and build the City Beautiful; and as we go forth on this mission, as good men go to far countries and lay down their lives in dark lands, let us ponder on His words for the poor and oppressed: 'Peter, feed my sheep.'"

These few quotations will show you more of the soul and character and lofty purpose of this woman than would a dozen chapters of ours.

It would be idle to record his replies to these strong and sincere appeals for man. Like a strong swimmer, borne forward by a strong, pure mountain torrent, he was entirely at her will. He asked nothing more, nothing better or higher, — only to help her help man; that was all in all to him.

How he worshipped her! And yet, she

ever seemed so far away. Once he dared to take her hand. She did not reprove him; she did not withdraw it, but he felt no response, such as he had hoped as some reward for his daring. What did her passive serenity mean?

V. — HOW BEAUTIFUL!

"How beautiful are the feet of those that preach the gospel of peace and bring glad tidings of good things!"

O star-built bridge, broad milky way!
   O star-lit, stately, splendid span!
If but one star should cease to stay
   And prop its shoulders to God's plan —
The man who lives for self, I say,
He lives for neither God nor man.

I count the columned waves at war
   With Titan elements; and they,
In martial splendor, storm the bar
   And shake the world, these bits of spray.
Each gives to each, and like the star
Gets back its gift in tenfold pay.

To get and give and give amain
   The rivers run and oceans roll.
O generous and high-born rain
   When raining as a splendid whole!
That man who lives for self, again,
I say, has neither sense nor soul.

WE have spoken of Miriam as a silent woman, for she really seemed silent at all times. She was, in fact, spoken of by all who knew her in London as the silent woman. And yet it will be seen that she said much. It may be that it is the man or woman who says nothing who is a great talker.

Socrates was a strangely silent man in his younger days, so far as we can find out; and yet he really said more than all the men and women of his century, so far as we know.

Jesus Christ was sad and silent at all times; and yet the things he said and suggested fill more books and find place in the hearts of more good people than the sayings of all the great men of earth put together.

Beauty, beauty of body and soul, was her idol. She kept the following lines from the Bible constantly before her:—

"Thou art beautiful, O my love, as Tirzah, comely as Jerusalem, terrible as an army with banners."

And here is another line she loved to repeat:—

"He hath made all things beautiful in his time."

Here follow some extracts from an epistle to Sir Moses Montifiore on his hundredth birthday:—

"All things are beautiful. All animate life is wondrously beautiful. You are beautiful; you were born beautiful,—beautiful in body as in soul; beautiful with the divine beauty and image of the Eternal. If this beauty of man shall be marred or scarred it will be the fault of man, not of his Maker. Time shall not touch nor tarnish man's beauty; man, only, can lay hand upon it. Man alone may make this beauty of body and of soul less perfectly beautiful than God made it at the first.

"It is a crime to make this beauty less beautiful. It is a duty to make this beauty daily more beautiful,—man's duty to himself, man's duty to his Maker, man's duty to man. It is man's duty to make his youth sweetly beautiful; it is man's duty to make his meridian of life magnificently beautiful; it is man's sacred duty to make his declining years, like your own, so serenely beautiful that man shall be in love with old age,—to be so tranquil, so perfectly at peace, so beautiful in body and in soul—a stately tree, Elijah's chariot of fire in the golden autumn—that men shall see a halo of light above the good, gray head as it goes down in the twilight to the River of Rest.

"'Ah, no, impossible!' sighs one; 'I cannot grow more beautiful daily, for I am daily trodden into the dust. I cannot even retain the beauty of body and of soul which God gave me to begin with.'

"I answer, look about you at the down-trodden grass. Resurgam! Resurgam! Look above you at the busy clouds, the battling elements.

There is not so very much rest anywhere, but there is beauty everywhere. Ay, I look down to the grass under my feet. The grass is daily trodden down, and yet it daily, hourly, tries to rise up, to grow and grow and be more beautiful even with its face in the dust. And when the storm comes it washes its face in the rain and rises up and again goes forward in its patient effort to make its one little place in man's pathway still more beautiful.

"Yes, it is to be conceded that there is not much rest for any one of us or for anything. All things toil. The oceans are busy building their sea-banks of shell and shale and snow-white sand and pretty, rounded pebbles. The flowers toil, the trees toil and toil and are often broken in mighty battles with the elements. All things toil and toil continually to make this beautiful world still more beautiful. And God himself, so far as we can find out, is the hardest toiler of all.

The thing to do is to toil harmoniously. Put the working world in harmony, and then work is rest. It is for this purpose, the purpose of possibly helping along in the line of harmony, that these thoughts, set down in the intervals of travel and toil of supervising, here in Palestine, the ploughing and planting, sowing grain or gathering fruit — it is in the hope of harmonizing and, maybe, the lighting of a lamp in one or two of the darker passes of life, as the peasants of Russia light lamps before the image of the Virgin in the dangerous passes of mountains, that I continually invoke the adoration of beauty.

"Meantime there is good reason for hope; for the world grows better, brighter, and more beautiful, vastly more beautiful year by year. So beautiful, indeed, has the world become that it almost seems that if man could only harmonize his forces, harmonize himself, with his surroundings, harmonize himself with himself, he could reach forth and say truly: 'The kingdom of heaven is at hand.'

"But, alas! we are a lot of garrulous children in a great, big boat in a great, big bay; and some row east and some row west, and some will not row at all, but live and thrive on the fears and misery and the despair of the weaker ones.

"But we must go forward and forward and forward, not around and around and around, as in all the centuries behind us. We must break this fatal circle. To this I consecrate my life."

VI. — THE SERMON ON THE MOUNT.

I think the birds in that far dawn
Were still. The bustling town below
Lay listening. Its strength was drawn
To him, as tides that inward flow.
   All Galilee lay still. Far fields of corn
   Lay still to hear that silent, sacred morn.

Be comforted; and blessed be
The meek, the merciful, the pure
Of heart; for they shall see, shall hear
God's mercy. So shall peace endure
   With God's peacemakers. They are His, and they
   Shall be His children in the Judgment Day.

THE great philanthropist had returned to London, leaving our two younger philanthropists and city-builders together in Jerusalem.

These two persons were together now almost entirely. They were absolute masters of their own time and work. They were under no legal obligation to any one. But what of that broader and far more binding moral obligation to man which goes with every gift of mental strength?

Being entirely released from all further care in Jerusalem, because the colonies in and round about the ancient cities had been trained, according to the wish of their founder, to lean on themselves, Miriam now began to look abroad.

As said before, she was far from satisfied that the best that could be done had been done here. It seemed to her like the same old story of going around and around and around; and she could not help seeing that every new generation would need a new Saviour and a new Sermon on the Mount. The same old enmities, the same old sorrows, and the same old sins.

There was a colony of Christians down by the sea not far from Joppa. The two city-builders went thither to see, to listen, and, if possible, to learn.

They found that these colonists had come to the Holy Land to pray and to await the coming of Christ. Their devout lives, their humility and continual habit of prayer appealed to the man greatly. But as for the woman, she had no patience with them.

"They should have gone to work in their own land, where God first set them down in the battle of life, and Christ would have been with them," she said.

"Why, how selfish!" she continued. "These few came here to await the second coming of Christ; as if they would be first to get into heaven."

"But they are so very devout."

"Yes, they prayed for rain all day and nearly all night last week, I am told; for their corn was being consumed by the fervor of the sun."

"And was not that a fine example of faith?"

"It was a fine example of folly, like all such prayers, and an exhibition of supreme selfishness. Why, they appealed to God to change a law of nature. They cried out to God all day and all night to send rain and ruin all the figs of Smyrna in order that they might have a dozen bags of corn! They simply prayed God to ruin fifty thousand people in order that fifty might have a little more green corn to eat! Selfishness like that cannot survive, and it should not."

He had never before seen her out of patience so entirely. It was evident that her plans for the salvation of the world, whatever they were, lay in line with the laws of nature. He began to learn that this boundless faith of hers was travelling hand in hand with reason. For while he, for his part, gave this colony of Christians all possible encouragement, and also a little solid assistance to help tide them through the trouble that was upon them because of the failure of corn, she gave neither consolation nor money. But instead, she gave the leader a letter to the British and American consuls, and directed him how to proceed to get his people home at her cost.

Half a year after the long prayer for rain, this colony, a sort of prayerful Brook Farm, was added to the list of similar failures, and the marsh grass now grows where the really devout and moral little community could not make corn to grow with all their prayers.

It is needless to say that this object-lesson in city-building here in the Holy Land was a sad discouragement to this man. Whatever her plans were, he, for his part, had planned something not very different from this. Only, he had not contemplated the turning back of man in his journey around the globe. He believed rather that all men should remain as nearly as possible at home, and begin the great reform in their own dooryard.

"Neither will that do," she said emphatically, as they sat by the Virgin's Fountain at Nazareth, whither they had gone as winter came on, and where they discussed this greatest problem of humanity.

"A well must be dug in the desert, and a great protecting tree be planted there. Of course, any good man will do his best; his hearthstone will be a holy altar on which he will lay his toil and example and life, and good children will grow from his good deeds. But a Jacob must rise up to dig a well by the way, and a Moses must come to lead up and out from the bondage of getting and getting and getting. There must be some great central beginning; and it must be removed, it must be remote from all these cruel and hard traditions of trade till, like a child, it has at least learned to stand alone. For, although the new-born city might be a Hercules at its birth, there would come, not only two serpents, but twenty serpents, to strangle it in its cradle."

This, the foregoing, is what she said one twilight as they sat on the now grass-grown escarpment of the hill above the holy little city, and in answer to his hint that they should build the City Beautiful there where they would have slain the Christ. And she said it so severely! She was almost cruel in her putting aside of his sentimental plans. Do or say what he could she seemed to grow further away from him day by day; and his earnest, honest heart was breaking for just one word. Was he so entirely of earth, or was it that she was so entirely of heaven, that he had not yet dared a second time to touch her hand?

VII. — IN THE SWEAT OF THY FACE.

What sound was that? A pheasant's whir?
　What stroke was that? Lean low thine ear.
Is that the stroke of carpenter,
　That far, faint echo that we hear?
Is that the sound that sometime Bedouins tell
Of hammer stroke as from his hand it fell?

It is the stroke of carpenter,
　Through eighteen hundred years and more
Still sounding down the hallowed stir
　Of patient toil; as when he wore
The leathern dress, — the echo of a sound
That thrills for aye the toiling, sensate ground.

Hear Mary weaving! Listen! Hear
　The thud of loom at weaving time
In Nazareth. I wreathe this dear
　Tradition with my lowly rhyme.
Believing everywhere that she may hear
The sound of toil, sweet Mary bends an ear.

Yea, this the toil that Jesus knew;
　Yet we complain if we must bear.
Are we more dear? Are we more true?
　Give us, O God, and do not spare!
Give us to bear as Christ and Mary bore
With toil by leaf-girt Nazareth of yore!

THESE rhymes tell in a crude way a pretty tradition of toil. It is the dove perhaps, the wood dove, which the half-wild sons of desolation and the desert have heard; for Nazareth is still the city of woods. The very name meant woods. Even now, as in the time of Jesus Christ, people of the city are saying, "Can any good thing come out of the woods — the West?"

To recount the plans of these two city-builders, here where Christ toiled, taught in the synagogue, and was dragged to the hilltop to be hurled down, would take long indeed. Let it be enough to say that they were seeking for light. "Light, more light!" was their one desire and demand.

"Life is so short!" she said one day. "For my part, I cannot afford to make a failure and die. That would be too terrible!" She paused long, and then with lifted face and clasped hands she said earnestly, "But to make a success, and then die — ah, that would be joy, joy, joy!"

At such times as this she seemed to him to be thousands of miles from his side. It is more than possible that a strong, pure, and complete woman may concentrate her entire soul and body to some high and holy purpose as well without taking either vow or veil as if she took both in all due form and solemnity.

Leaving Nazareth, they journeyed on

down into Egypt, taking the same way, as nearly as possible, as that by which Moses had come when leading his people toward the Holy Land.

One single incident of this journey, which might well fill a book, must be recorded; for it not only indicates something of her courage and strength of devotion but also tells something of her strange belief in not only the brotherhood of man but of all animate life.

They were tented for the night in the desert to the south of Mount Sinai when a lion approached almost to the tent door. As she calmly put her terrified servants behind her and, without a word, stepped between the man and the crouching beast, she looked it firmly in the face and said: —

"Why, don't you know me? I remember you, my brother, after all these ages." And she moved forward and would have laid her hand upon the lion's tumbled mane had he not drawn back and away to the sombre bosom of his mother, Night.

Yes, "I seem to remember all this now. I surely saw that lion long, long ago, and loved him," she said to the man at last, looking out and away to the holy mountain.

"And you have been here before?"

"Yes, yes, when Moses passed this way, thousands of years back, I was here. I remember it all as if it were but yesterday."

The journeys on the Nile, Karnak — all these are old, old. Let us go forward to the building of the new.

He had hoped somehow that in this warm land she would be nearer to him. She could not be dearer. She was his divinity, but she grew more distant, daily more distant. Or rather let us say simply she grew, daily grew in grandeur of soul, grew in goodness and unselfishness; and so, like a growing tree, was daily growing above him and beyond his touch or possible reach.

VIII. — THE CHRIST IN EGYPT.

O land of temples, land of tombs!
  O tawny land, O lion dead!
O silent land of silent looms ;
  Of kingly garments torn to shred!
O land of storied wonder still, as when
Fair Joseph stood the chiefest of all men!

  .   .   .   .   .   .

The Christ in Egypt! Egypt and
  Her mystic star-built Pyramids!
Her shoreless, tiger seas of sand!
  Her Sphynx with fixed and weary lids!
Her red and rolling Nile of yellow sheaves
Where Moses cradled 'mid his lily leaves.

Her lorn, dread temples of the dead
  Had waited, as mute milestones wait
By some untraversed way unread,
  Until the King, or soon or late,
Should come that tomb-built way and silent pass
To read their signs above the sand-sown grass.

Behold! Amid this majesty
  Of ruin, at the dust-heaped tomb
Of vanity came Christ to see
  Earth's emptiness, the dark death room
Of haughtiness, of kingly pomp, of greed,
Of gods of gold or stone, or storied creed.

And this His first abiding-place!
  And these dread scenes His childhood's toys!
What wonder at that thoughtful face?
  That boy face never yet a boy's?
What wonder that the elders marvelled when
A boy spake in the Temple unto men?

WHEN the perfect woman comes — and she will come — she will appeal to the soul of man, not to his body; and then the perfect man will not be far off.

Wherever this majestic and beautiful woman was, — this piteously beautiful woman, whatever she was yet to be or may have been, — she seemed to be, from the first time we encountered her at Jerusalem, entirely unconscious of sex. She seemed not to be a body, but a soul; and a soul, as said before, that was growing daily, as a great magnolia flower-tree grows, with its perfect flowers and its soft, warm, sensuous perfume, widening, warming day by day till it fills the garden, turns all faces to this one flower-tree, draws all things to itself, and drowns all senses but this one sense of perfume and the perfection of form and color.

As they had descended through the deserts and wilderness, and, as before noted, had retraced the ancient path by which Israel had gone up out of Egypt, she seemed to this man who companioned her, followed her afar off, to be all-powerful.

There is a lone obelisk where stood the city of Om, famous as the place where Plato and others of the wise men studied philosophy, — one lone obelisk; and that is all you can see to-day of the storied city of Om, where, it is still whispered, men gathered together who knew all things, — even to the secrets that were before life and are after death.

Some palm trees stood not far away, and the two sat on a toppled granite column in silence there together as the sun was going down on tawny, tired, and prostrate Egypt.

"Oh to see Egypt rise up and stand erect in her splendor once more before the end of the world!" He said this at last, as the sun lay level on the red waters of the Nile, and dashed the world with molten gold.

Was it a sense of pain that tinged her face, — displeasure, effort, exhaustion, something such as Christ felt as he turned to the woman when she touched the hem of His garment? Or was it a sense of his own unworthiness which made him to imagine that a faint tinge of displeasure swept over her face as she lifted it to the waters, and in silence put forth her hand as she arose?

Who shall say? And what matter? His eyes, as he sprang to his feet, followed the direction of her hand, and there, before his startled vision, in all her storied splendor of dome, citadel, and battlement, grove.

garden, turret, and tower, that melted into the hazy horizon and filled all the face of the earth as far as the eye could sweep, lay ancient Egypt. Describe the scene? The attempt would be profanity. Account for this power of hers? When science will come forward and account for the cities, seas, forests, armies of marching heroes with banners and battle harness, that men see almost daily for themselves on the plains and deserts of America, without even the presence of any finer organization than their own to call up these visions of the past, then will it be time enough to give some reasons here.

As her wearied hand fell to her side, she sank back; all Egypt of old fell down and lay again in dust beneath her pyramids. He felt that now she was as far away from him and above him and beyond him, as was the farthest and loftiest column she had recalled to existence. He sighed as they turned in silence home. He now began to see his uselessness and his helplessness in her presence. All the manhood in the man began to rise in self-assertion. He grew more firmly resolved than ever to go forth alone and meditate and purify his soul, go up in the mountains to pray, as did the prophets of old, till he, too, had Faith.

IX. — AWAITING THE RESURRECTION AT KARNAK.

Lorn land of silence, land of awe!
   Lorn, lawless land of Moslem will, —
The great Law-giver and the law
   Have gone away together. Still
The sun shines on ; still Nilus darkly red
Steals on between his awful walls of dead.

And sapphire skies still bend as when
   Proud Karnak's countless columns propped
The corners of the world; when men
   Kept watch where massive Cheops topped
Their utmost reach of thought, and sagely drew
Their star-lit lines along the trackless blue.

But Phthah lies prostrate evermore ;
   And Thoth and Neith all are gone ;
And huge Osiris hears no more,
   Thebes' melodies ; nor Mut at On ;
Yet one lone obelisk still lords the spot
Where Plato sat to learn. But On is not.

Nor yet has Time encompassed all;
   You trace your finger o'er a name
That mocks at age within the wall
   Of fearful Karnak. Sword nor flame
Shall touch what men have journeyed far to touch
And felt eternity in daring such !

"Juda Melchi Shishak ! " Read
   The Holy Book ; read how that he
With chariot and champing steed
   Invaded far and fair Judea.
Yea, read the chronicle of red hands laid
   On " shields of gold which Solomon had made."

HE would look once more upon Upper Egypt through her eyes, and then away about his work. She was so infinitely above him that he could only clasp his hands and with lifted face worship her; he could worship her from afar as well as near at hand. He could not love her more, though he sat at her feet forever, and walked at her side even through the shadows of the valley of death. He would not, he could not, love her less though millions of miles away.

Did I forget to tell you that her singularly intense and perfect mentality took in and absorbed to herself the minds, the inmost thoughts of those who came in contact with her? She knew men's thoughts, — may I say it, with humbled head? — as Christ knew men's thoughts.

"There is a tomb, a mighty tomb, not far from here," — and this was at Karnak that she now spoke, — " which no man has entered since long, long before Christ came to Egypt, and this you should see."

She had been talking of his going, of his plans, his purposes, — talking to him in the same clear, sweet way as in Jerusalem and at Nazareth, that morning. And yet he had said nothing at all of these things to her for a long time.

Knowing that she knew his heart, his hopes, his plans, how quietly good, patient, and true he had begun to grow! And why should he tell her anything, since she knew all and more than all that he could possibly find words to utter in all the centuries that are to be? Why shall time be wasted in helpless, inane, and angular words at all? Let us rather learn to read the soul in silence, and respect it.

Their boat was rocking on the Nile as night came on; and, as the Arabs slowly rowed for the sandy shore, which she had indicated with her hand as the place of the hidden tomb, she said to the man at her side, in her quiet and fragmentary way:—

"Yes, Christ surely raised the dead. And do you not see that Egypt anticipated all that? She believed, she knew that some one would some day walk this way so full of the fires of life and immortality, so charged with that finer electricity that men call life, about which they talk so much but about which they know nothing at all, as yet,— that they laid their dead away ready to rise up in all their glory on earth after their long waiting for the Master."

More, much more she said; and all so much more intelligently than what is here so imperfectly recalled and written down!

It was a woful, grewsome spot of bone and stone, of sand and serpents, where they landed, and all tracked about with the tracks of wide-footed and enormous lions. And they had to stoop low, almost kneel, to enter the mouth of the cavern. There was no sign of man's hand or foot, although she had come to it as if walking a beaten road.

He had looked back and down to the men as he stooped to enter the gloomy cavern. The Arabs had anchored in the middle of the river, — were they afraid of lions? It was soon dark as they passed on and on in a stooping posture; but she assured him that in a little time they would find the cavern lighted. With calm assurance she said that when the great founder of Babylon had been laid to rest there, thousands of years before, the walls were left lighted ; no, not with electricity, but with a phosphorescent light that must endure while the Nile endures.

But it was wearisome, stooping and groping so long and so far. He began to fear that she had made some miscalculation and was lost. There were other and deeper passes and many tunnels that intersected this dark and narrow one. He could feel them as he groped forward after her, — feel them, not altogether with his hands, but with that other and finer feeling which she had, by example, begun to teach him. She paused, put out her hand, took his in hers for the first time since that first meeting in Jerusalem. But now her hand trembled,— it was almost cold. Had she indeed lost her way? Had she, with her superhuman knowledge and divine gifts, really lost her way in that awful wilderness of tombs? Had she at last lost her strength, her faith? Suddenly she stopped short, and said, "There is a lion in here."

The man tried to stand erect and take some attitude of defence, if only to encourage her. There was not room to rise erect.

But now her blood began to tide and flow again. Her hand was warm once more and her heart strong. "We will go forward," she said as she again led the way, "for to go back will be to invite destruction. He is not far away; I think he is waiting in one of the side passes. There!"

Her hand was again like ice, but only for a time. They stood leaning, looking forward in the fearful darkness at two glittering lights, round, full, flaming lights that broadened and brightened and gleamed and glowed with a fierceness, a hungry, animal fierceness that you could feel. It was something more than light, it was heat. It was heat that chilled, turned you cold and froze you to the marrow. The man, although trained to the use of arms, and not without address in danger, had, ever since coming into her higher atmosphere, despised their use; and so here he stooped and groped, as helpless and unmanned as a babe.

But her old faith came back, even as she looked into the burning fires before her, and with a pressure of her warm hand she led forward. The pass widened now and was roomier in every way. It soon became a sort of court, great columns of red and gray and blue granite propping the mountains above. On the outer edge of this court lay the huge lion, his nose on his paws, his eyes, his terribly beautiful eyes only, giving the least sign of life or action. But for those eyes of fire and flame, he, too, might have been counted as one of the thousand images that kept attendance on the great Babylonian who sat his throne in robes of state in the vast, wide court far beyond.

That distant inner court was still lighted, as she had said, after all the thousands of years; and there the mighty hunter of Babylon had sat his golden and marble and granite throne as time rolled by, resting and resting and serenely waiting the resurrection. The shapely columns, in all their comeliness and strength, stood out before the far-off light in stately splendor.

Miriam did not pause for one moment. She held the man's hand tight and close, to make certain that he, too, should keep right on as she might lead. The lion did not move; he did not even lift his eyes as they drew near. But suddenly his tail whipped slightly in the dust; then the woman led a little to the left, leaving a column between her path and the paws of the lion. The huge beast seemed pleased with this slight concession; and only noting that they kept straight on, knowing surely that there was but one way out and that he was thrown full length in the only path of exit, he awaited results with that dignity which is born of boundless strength and absolute assurance. He could afford to wait just a little.

"Yes, here is faith for you; certainty of immortality on earth. Look! Nimrod, the mighty hunter, armed and ready for battle with beasts of the forest, as of old! He has only been resting here all these centuries, ready to rise up and begin life again just as he left off when he lay down to die; as we all shall."

She had forgotten the lion in this supreme moment to which she had looked forward so long, and, possibly at times, with some doubt. But she was now certain that Egypt had been not only the mother of all ancient civilization, but the mother of Babylon's founder and the burial-place of her mighty dead for ages.

Reverently she approached the foot of the lofty throne and kneeled on the polished red granite below, where reached the staff, the long beam of the hunter's spear, still clutched in his right hand, and ready for use when he should rise again.

How long they meditated there, in that soft and hallowed light and holy perfume of the past, no one can say. There are times that despise time, that throw time away as a drunken spendthrift throws coins away; and there is an intoxication of the soul and senses at times like this that puts the intoxication of the body, even from the rarest wines, to the blush.

Suddenly there was a low, slow, deep rumble. It seemed as if the cavern, or court of the kingly dead, began to rock, and roll, and shake and tremble; then a roar!

It rolled, bounded, echoed, rebounded, filled the place and all places, all the passes, got lost, could not find its way out, came back, bounded from wall to wall, from floor to ceiling, and finally went back and moaned and died in that lion's monstrous jaws and tawny mane.

He rose up, came forward, and then, as if he had only been jesting at first in a sort of suppressed whisper, he roared again, again and again.

Five steps of polished red granite of the throne of the mighty dead with spear in hand; but they made it at a single bound, she to the left and he to the right.

The man was about to pluck the spear from the dark and dusty hand and do battle for the woman he deified; but she looked him in the face across the face of the king, and he bowed his head and stepped back in silence, as her now burning hand reached further and fell familiarly on the outstretched left hand of the mighty hunter where it rested on the arm of the throne.

Was it a halo about her head? Was it divine fire that flamed from her burning hand? Nay, no questions. They cannot be answered here. We may only know that some subtle essence — fire? magnetism? electricity? — flowed and swept and shot from her hand, from her body, to his body. And then the mighty hunter was on his feet. As the lion laid his long, strong paw on the third step of the throne, with his tail whipped back in the air and his two terrible hinder legs bent low and gathered for a leap at the woman's throat, the spear was in place; face to face the lion and his master, once more and at last after all these thousands of years! And the lion knew his master. He knew him only from tradition; but the story of his powers had come down to him with his very blood, and he knew his kingly master when he met him, even in the house of death.

Sullenly, slowly, and with a dignity worthy the occasion and the two mighty kings, the lion dragged, dragged, as if he had to drag it down by force, that great, ponderous paw. It literally tore the granite, but he got it down. He got his eyes down from the eyes of the dead; and then sidewise, slowly, gracefully, grandly, with long and stately strides, only the quivering of his flanks telling of his anger, he bowed his head and left the court and crept from the fearful cavern. And when they had ceased to look and listen to make certain he was surely gone, the dead was sitting there as at first.

X.—THE VOICE OF TOIL.

Come, lean an ear, an earnest ear,
   To Nature's breast, some stilly eve,
And you shall hear, shall surely hear
   The Carpenter, and shall believe;
Shall surely hear, shall hear for aye, who will,
The patient strokes of Christ resounding still.

The thud of loom, the hum of wheel,
   That steady stroke of carpenter!
And was this all? Did God reveal
   No gleam of light to Him, to her?
No gleam of hopeful light, sweet toiling friend,
Save that which burneth dimly at the end.

That beggar at the rich man's gate!
   That rich man moaning down in hell!
And all life's pity, all life's hate!
   Yea, toil lay on Him like a spell.
Stop still and think of Christ, of Mary there,
Her lifted face but one perpetual prayer.

I can but hope at such sore time,
   When all her soul went out so fond,
She touched the very stars sublime
   And took some sense of worlds beyond;
And took some strength to ever toil and wait
The glories bursting through God's star-built gate.

And He so silent, patient, sad,
   As seeing all man's sorrows through!
How could the Christ be wholly glad
   To know life's pathos as He knew,—
To know, and know that all the beauteous years
Man still will waste in battle, blood, and tears?

Enough of antiquity, of dust, and of the dead; enough of speculation, of groping in the darkness and of guess-work; enough of idleness. Turn we now to toil. Enough, and more than enough of the old; turn we now to the new, — to follow the stroke of the Carpenter's Son, the sound of Mary's loom, or the voice of the dove in the olive-trees.

But one word before bidding a long adieu to the old world and this strange, strong woman of the old.

I do not say or even suggest that she was the reincarnation of that Miriam who was made "leprous white" because of her anger with her brother when he married "the Ethiopian woman." I know nothing at all about such things. But I am permitted to believe that our business is with this world mainly, and with the things of this world; that other worlds have their own, and are and ought to be concerned mainly with their own; that it is a fact and a very practical fact, that "the kingdom of heaven is at hand."

Immortality? Certain of it. But it is here. Individuality in the next life? Certain of it, if a grain and not a husk. As no atom of earth perishes, so shall no soul perish or lose its personality. The real acorn, the real grain of wheat does not perish or lose its identity in dust. It is only the worthless grain and the husk and shell that passes back to the common mould.

So, then, if you want immortality, make it. If you want your soul saved, make it worth saving.

These thoughts, bear in mind, are not intruded upon any one, and are but timidly and feebly let fall here as " the still, small rain."

A LARGE solemnity like twilight, almost like night, had settled down on Miriam and the man also, on their return to the vicinity of Cairo. He knew that work was now before him, and he was glad of that. But would she be at his side? There could be no toil to weary where she was. There could be no rest, no light, no life, nothing for him where she was not.

He tried to be very honest with himself, with her. But think it all over as he might, recall each act and utterance, yet in all their intercourse he could find nothing on which to hang a hope that she would be with him to the end, — be his own. And then she was so silent, so sadly silent of late, all the time.

True, she was not strong, strong of body; for as her soul grew strong her body grew weak. Even little threads of silver had wound themselves through her heavy meshes of midnight hair, and her glorious face was wan and pallid as the moonlight in which they sat by the deep-red Nile this last night in Egypt. But he loved her all the more for that. The more? — how could that have been? Let us say with a tenderness that was new and holy.

But his heart was bursting for some sight, some sound. Would she let him go, and go alone, with no assurance that she would follow and follow soon, — be with him in heart, and soul too, all the time?

He would put the matter to the test at once. As we have seen, he was not given to words any more than was she.

"You know I love you, Miriam."

"I know."

"And you?"

Her two hands lifted up and pushed back the great mass of black hair from her fine, white face, and it came out to him like the moon of heaven, and with her face turned full to his she said, slowly, softly, and so very sweetly, —

"I love you, John Morton."

It was the first time she had spoken his name so, his plain, simple name.

The hands remained above and about the face, framing it like a face of the Madonna.

"You, you will be mine?"

"Yes."

"God bless you, Miriam, for that promise. But you know I go now to begin my work in the New World. When will you be mine? Where? At what time?"

"Time?" Her hands fell down and lay so heavily in her lap he dared not try to touch them, and she said, looking away beyond, as if at the ghost of Thebes and her hundred gates, "Time? Not in time — eternity."

He sprang up and threw his arms tightly together across his breast.

"And this is your resolution?"

"Why, dare I be idly happy with all this misery of earth before me? Think of that blind woman with the three naked children yesterday in the street; she had the arms and the mummy-head of some ancestor, selling them for a bit of bread, here in fruitful Egypt! For them, no blame. They know no better. You and I know better. 'For unto whomsoever much is given, of him shall be much required.' The cross and the crown are bound together. Let us go our ways, help to make the crooked straight, and then, in some after life — "

Her voice was inaudible now. Her face sank low and was hidden from his sight; but he saw hot tears falling on her hand; and she was sacred and holy to him as if a halo had descended upon her.

Then she rose up slowly, her face still bent down, and giving her two hands, said:

"Go; do your work, do good."

"And you?"

"I, I will come to you — sometime; but go, go now."

What a tower, what a pillar of fire was that promise: "I will come to you — sometime! Go, go now. I will come to you — sometime. Good-by!"

It was a Nile night. To those who have lived by the Nile nothing more need be said to describe the sensuous scene and air. To those who have not dwelt there the description would be as idle as ungrateful. There were palm trees in the ancient garden by which the lion-like river crept in all his sinuous and supple splendor. The moon made little paths and patches and quivering mosaics of silver all up and down the sands to walk upon.

A boat with a single oarsman rocked and

rested in the lotus leaves by the level bank above, and at the end of the garden a single nude, black boatman. It was a very quiet place. No boat had landed there in all the time they had lived here.

He turned away, passed down the garden with slow step, empty-handed, alone, and with the one word "Good-by" on his lips. They could not have uttered more than that one word. His resolution was almost failing him, for his heart was breaking. Then suddenly he turned about, flew back to her, threw out his hands and cried, "Good-by, Miriam!"

Mechanically and slowly and with kindly eyes and half-parted lips, she took his outstretched hands in silence. He pulled her to him, pulled her violently, pressed her to his heart as his right hand swept swiftly about her body, pressed his lips to her proud lips as she struggled and as her head fell back in her effort to escape; and then he set her hastily in her place and was gone.

Intensely, triumphantly beat his heart as he leaped into his boat, sped away, and hastened to embark for other lands. And long, long, as he voyaged away, he tried to believe, tried to hope, that there had been at least the faintest thrill of response, and that he had not been entirely a savage.

XI. — THE FOUNDATION STONES.

Be thou not angered. Go thy way
   From God's high altar to thy foe;
Nor think to kneel and truly pray,
   Till thou art reconciled and know
Thou hast forgiven him; as thou must be
Forgiven of the sins that burthen thee.

And if thine eye tempt thee to shame
   Turn thou aside; pluck it away!
And with thy right hand deal the same,
   Nor tempt thy soul to sin this day.
Yea, thou art very weak. Thou couldst not make
One hair turn white or black, for thine own sake.

And whosoever smite thy cheek,
   Turn thou that he may smite again.
The truly brave are truly meek,
   And bravely bear both shame and pain.
They slay, if truly brave men ever slay,
Their foes, with sweet forgiveness, day by day.

And if a man would take thy coat,
   Give him thy cloak and count it meet.
Bread cast on waters can but float
   In sweet forgiveness to thy feet;
So thou, by silent act like this, shalt preach
Such sermons as not flame nor sword can teach.

Lay not up treasures for yourselves
   On earth, and stint and starve the soul
By heaping granaries and shelves
   And high store-houses; for the whole
Of wealth is this: to grow and grow and grow
In faith; to know and ever seek to know.

Therefore give not too much of thought
   For thy to-morrows. Birds that call
Sweet melodies sow not, reap not,
   And yet the Father feedeth all.
Therefore toil trusting, loving; watch and pray,
And pray in secret; pray not long, but say:

Give us our daily bread this day,
   Forgive our sins as we forgive,
Lead us not in temptation's way,
   Deliver us, that we may live;
For thine the kingdom is, has ever been,
And thine the power, the glory, and — Amen!

ON a huge mass of hills, hills heaped and banked and tumbled on top of hills by the great sea of seas, and above the Golden Gate, the man at last pitched his tent and began to build his city.

Water percolated through the broken rocks here and there and formed little pools, where poor, half-starved cattle and sheep had gathered for half a century and made dismal moan for provender as they trampled the rich, black mould into unsightly masses of mud.

It was a doleful, grewsome place indeed, if you looked near about you or down into the mud. But to look up to the stars! To look down to the bay of San Francisco; look out through the Golden Gate on the great sea, to count the moving ships, to behold the fleets of snow-white clouds that drew in at the sunset from the Japan seas, to feel the keen, cool winds of Alaska in July! Ah, it was a glorious place if you could only keep your face toward the sea or up toward heaven, and your heart in your duty to man.

And what heaps of stone! — stones from the topmost peak of his hundred acres to the bottom limit of his possessions; stones enough for the material foundations of a large city indeed! As for its moral foundations, no city ever has been built, or ever can be built, to endure with any other than the precepts at the head of this chapter, — the Sermon on the Mount.

Of course it would have been a pleasant thing if this man could have chosen a rich valley by some great river, where commerce, in the spirit of the age, and enterprising people with quick discernment of advantage would come his way at once. It would be pleasant to write down the peace and rest and swift prosperity that would have followed such a choice of location. But we have ugly facts, not pleasant fancy, to confront and deal with now.

The man took the mountain-top, and at the cost of all he had saved in more than half a lifetime, simply because a place in the valley was not to be had for what he had to give.

"All the better," he said. "If I succeed on these steeps and heaps of stone, the greater good and the braver will be my lesson to the world. The main thing is to teach and to prove that all men are good or trying to be good; and that all the world and all things in it are beautiful or trying to be beautiful. I shall plant roses here where I find thorns, fruit where I find thistles; and if I can make this most barren and most unsightly of all places on earth beautiful, my example will not be lost." And his heart was all the time with *Her*, and all the time he kept saying over and over her last words: "I will come to you — sometime."

His heap of steep hills sloped to the sun and the sea; but back in the rear a deep and wooded and watered canyon bent like a scimitar and shut out all the world behind him. It was a wild and a glorious place; wolves, catamounts, hosts of wild creatures housed there, to say nothing of the birds that sang and reared their pretty broods in the redwood groves and groves of madrona, willow, and bay trees. But he built his little house out in the sun with the Golden Gate in sight, and here he began to plant trees, and to plant and to plant and to plant. He would first make it attractive, and then invite thinkers, poets, men of mind who had a mind to rest, to come and sit down and share it with him; then the world would see and learn and live. Then *She* would come! And why did he begin and toil on so entirely alone? He did not begin alone; or did not propose to do that at first.

He had found, after much care, a small party of men with purposes not unlike his own. But when it came to the toil, the privations, the weary prospect of long waiting for roads to be built, for trees to grow up and bear fruit, for the world to come that way and admire and praise, they melted away, one after one, and went down to the city by the sea and left him all alone. It would be tedious, even if it would be credible, to tell how terribly hard he toiled. But there was fierce excitement in closing in and making clean the muddy springs of water, in training the pure, trickling streams down the tortuous new roadside where roses were newly set by the newly built wall. To see the response of the roses! real gratitude indeed! And then the down-trodden grass — how glad it was to lift up its head after forty years!

But then at last he must have help. He could earn a little in various little ways, and would employ some one to help him in his persistent toil. But whom?

When we employ a man we must not think entirely of ourselves. We must think of his good as well as our own. He needs this consideration.

From far across San Pablo Bay, the lights from the watch-towers of the Penitentiary shot sharp and continuously in at the door of our silent city-builder. This vexed him sorely at first. It made him miserable to think of the misery there when he so needed rest.

But at last his soul ascended to the duty before it. He went to the prison warden and engaged that each month he should send him the first discharged convict who desired work. The first to come was a poor drunkard. It was not quite an ideal life, this sleeping in the same little room with an illiterate drunkard. True, the poor, sullen inebriate did not know that his history was known to the city-builder, but still he was ugly and cross. He did not like the place; and so he soon disappeared, taking what he could lay hands on.

The next was a bright young man who

had been a book-keeper, and stolen money from his employer.

Thinking his history unknown, he frankly told it the first night. They became friends. When he drew his first wages he went down into the city, into the sea, as it were, and was drowned, — drowned first in alcohol and then found dead in the bay.

The third was a witless man and an honest man, who insisted on telling his story, hat in hand, before he would sit down. He had been convicted of stealing cattle, and did not assert his innocence till he stood with his month's wages in his hand to set out for the gold mines of Alaska.

Taken altogether, these experiments were in no way fruitless nor discouraging. But the man's little hoard was expended. Now and again he wrought entirely alone. And as he toiled, he took the three convicts and their conduct under the closest consideration. And the prayer of Jesus Christ, the one prayer, as taught him by that clear-eyed woman from the gates of Jerusalem, kept in his mind and before him always: "Lead us not into temptation! Lead us not into temptation! Lead us not into temptation!"

He had tempted the first unhappy convict

to fall. The poor, weak-minded, and sullen man could not resist the temptation to take the man's horse and ride away in the night. He was, then, himself the guilty man.

As for the second man, he, too, had been tempted, — tempted even to his death by Society and the State.

As for the third man, no better had been found. Indeed, very many worse men than he had been encountered.

By this time vultures began to gather around and sit on the rocks. They said: "This man with his non-resistance and turn-the-other-cheek must fail, die; and some one must pick his bones."

This was an ugly fact, but who was to blame? "Be ye wise as serpents, but as harmless as doves."

Would a really wise man have come forward and publicly and continuously declared, in the midst of a people who were devoted entirely to money-getting, that he would give to the man who took his coat, his cloak also?

He was tempting some weak men beyond their power to resist. He was literally calling out to the vultures to come from the four parts of the world and wait on the rocks and crags for him to die, when they should gorge on his remains.

People came and went as the years went by, — some queer people, some curious people, and some good people; or rather some people who had had better fortune, better opportunities to be good than those who are called bad.

"Now, look here!" said an honest and observing man one day to the city-builder, digging on his hill, "all this that you are trying to do has been done before, or at least attempted. You are, perhaps, a good man, a very good man; but you are not the only good man that has been. You may build and build, but the sea of selfishness will roll over your city and all your enterprises here when you die, before you can be carried to the grave."

This had been said in answer to his complaints about the vultures that continually hovered around. He had, in his distress, cried out to this good man, and said : —

"In the olden time the ravens fed the prophets; but now it seems to me that the prophets must feed not only the ravens but the vultures also."

And it must be conceded that he had the most substantial reasons for complaining.

For example : A stout German, whose lands shut him out from the city, nailed up his road, and demanded an acre of land for the right of way. The man gave him a deed of three acres. But this is only one example of his folly and the persistence of the vultures, and we hasten on.

And yet these people on this mountainside were in some sense better than those in the valley below, and those in the valley below were better than those in the city beyond.

How pitiful, how piteously pitiful it all is, as things now are! This man, worn out at last, bodily and mentally, sat down and tried to see light beyond. There was no light to be seen. He saw that he would ultimately be ground to dust between the hard and selfish elements that environed him. He might carry his experiments forward to the end of his own natural life; he might not be crucified before his time to die; yet he foresaw clearly that his very dust and ashes would be divided among those about him at his death, and all his hopes and plans and persistent toil of body and mind would be in a day as if he had never been.

He began to search the book of Nature for some possible solution of the hard problem before him; and he began to see that Nature had in some way or other protected whatever she wished to perpetuate. Even the timid rabbit, that sat with wide eyes and large ears under the trees which he had planted on his hillsides, was not neglected. His coat turned gray each season as the grass turned gray; and when the winter approached, with a sprinkle of snow on the hillside, the keen-eyed hawk that looked down out of the snow-cloud above saw that the rabbit had a new coat as white as the snows about him, and that it required the keenest of keen eyes to distinguish him from the tufts of grass and snow.

"Yet I," said the man to himself, " with all the lessons of Nature before me, have dared to lay my breast bare to all men; and they have pierced me through and through."

One day a small man, with a gray beard, came up the hill meekly washing his hands, and in a mild and sympathetic voice said:

"You seem discouraged. Let me assist you. I have watched you and your work with the deepest interest, and now that you seem so weary I have come to save you. Yes, I am a real-estate agent. There are too many real-estate agents in the town, — three hundred of them. There are nearly two hundred lawyers; there are more than fifty preachers; there are twice as many doctors, — all living on a small city. But I have come to save you. I will sell some of your land. This will give you money to go ahead. I have your permission?"

The small, gray man had not paused for answer, nor did he wait for a single word, but again washing his hands, and smiling again his sickly smile, and still talking on in a soft and sympathetic tone, he crept backward, and crawled like a serpent down the hill to sell the land.

Now, there is nothing in this incident worth telling. The only excuse for it is the ugly truth that these idle, cunning men, made desperate by competition, are crowding every city, and plying their trade to the very verge of crime, — most miserable themselves and making others miserable. What a jar of Egyptian vipers is the heart and soul of society to-day!

XII. — THE FIRST LAW OF GOD.

> Look back, beyond the Syrian sand,
>   Beyond the awful flames that burst
> O'er Sinai! That first command
>   Outside the gates, God's very first,
> Was this: "Thou shalt in sweat and constant toil
> Eat bread till thou returnest to the soil."

"YOU have a rough place here, it seems to me," said a man with bag and gun and dog as he came around a crag up out of the canyon one evening. There was a tone of derision in the voice of the hunter. He was from the city, and seemed to think the man who was trying to plant a little olive-tree in a cleft of the crag ought to not only let him have the shooting of the birds, but a better road to flush them from.

Our city-builder was weary, and for a moment was angry. But lifting his face from his work he laid the little olive by, and slowly straightening his back he looked the man in the face, and then looked about and above, and then said quietly as he did so, "Yes, yes, it is rough under foot; but it is as smooth overhead as any man's land."

The hunter whistled to his dog, and left the man with the little olive-tree alone in his clouds. For he did not understand; and we are always afraid of that which we do not understand.

The lonely man on the peak kept on planting his olive-trees in the clouds. He thought of the dove bringing an olive-branch in its beak, "plucked off," and reflected that the ancients must have planted their loftiest peaks in olive-trees and made them flourish, and so took heart a little. He finished planting his tree, and being very weary and very lonely he lay down by his mattock, with his face to the glorious Balboa seas below, and thought of Jacob on the plains of Shinar as he pillowed his head on a stone and slept and dreamed.

  Lo! on the plains of Bethel lay
   An outworn lad, unhoused, alone,
  His couch the tawny mother clay,
   His pillow that storm-haunted stone;
  The hollow winds howled down the star-lit plain,
  All white and wild with highborn wintry rain.

  Yet here God's ladder was let down,
   Yea, only here for aye and aye!
  Not in the high-walled, splendid town,
   Not to the throned king feasting high,
  But far beneath the storied Syrian stars
  God's ladder fell from out the golden bars.

And ever thus. Take heart! to some
  The hand of fortune pours her horn
Of plenty, smiling where they come;
  And some to wit and some to wealth are born,
And some are born to pomp and splendid ease;
But lo! God's shining ladder leans to none of these.

The German neighbor on the hillside below saw the weary dreamer through the rift of clouds that came driving in from the sea with the stars, and kindly came up the peak and awoke him.

"It won't pay you to plant olive-trees here. Why do you do this?"

"To make my little portion of the world more beautiful."

"Boh! I don't believe in beauty; dot don't pay."

"Then you do not believe in God?"

"Vell, not in dot sort of a God nohow."

This German had been amazed at the man's deeding him so much more land than he had demanded. He thought it was a mistake at first; and so for months had said nothing. But at last he could conceal his curiosity no longer. Leaning over the shoulder of the man from whom he had received it, one Sunday as he sat reading, he said: —

"My lawyer, he say when a deed is

recorded it is done with and no one can change it. So that matter is settled between us. You owe me notting, and I owe you notting. But tell me why you made it three instead of one."

Slowly the man opened the Book at the Sermon on the Mount and quietly proceeded to read. He paused a moment when he came to the 31st verse; then he read in a slow, low, and kindly voice, and closing the book, he looked his neighbor calmly in the face and repeated: "And if a man will sue thee at law and take away thy coat, let him have thy cloak also."

Now this big, hearty German was not a bad man; he was, in fact, far from a bad man as the world goes. But this strange new man had tempted him, and the end was not yet.

Meantime the people for his city, to people his city, did not come, save to look on curiously and go away. The City Beautiful was building slowly indeed.

At last one man with much money came and proposed to build and abide, with all his household.

"And you are certain it will pay me?"

"Perfectly certain that it will pay you immensely, sir."

"Well, if you are so certain I can make money — "

"Stop! Who said money? I said it will pay you. But to make money here on these rocks! Why, you might as well try to plant God's altar in corn, or to grow wheat on the pinnacle of Saint Paul's cross, as to make money on these glorious heights. No; you would be paid, but you would take your pay from the heaped-up gold of the golden sunsets of the Golden Gate; from the silver banks of clouds beyond; from the certificates of perfect health from the far-off Japan seas; from the satisfaction of having built or helped to build one, just one, City of Refuge, where the Jews had so many. From these and the like of these you would be paid ten thousand fold, my friend, but you would make no money."

"Well, I will think it over, and I may come back."

He did not come back; and so the world kept on going by the other way. True, crowds came oftentimes, — carriages and carriages, on Sundays; for the drives were good, the air delicious, the spectacle of the seas and cities below divinely glorious. But with the exception of a painter, a poet, a traveller who came to rest for a few days, the City Beautiful continued to be uninhabited.

Finally a friend in Japan sent two little Japanese gentlemen from Tokio, to serve him, to be his companions, to hear his philosophy, to learn his interpretation of the story and teachings of Christ. And this was good! "At last, at last!" said the hermit.

On the third day after they came a big Irishman and his followers came to the hermit's cottage.

"We are a committee," said the leader, "for the protection of white labor. You are a laboring man, and of course will stand by white labor. The Japs must go, or they will get the worst of it."

The man tried to protest, but all his protestations were of no avail. The foreigners said their children would stone the Japanese as they went up and down the road if they did not leave. John Morton told his two little strangers all, and they quietly and with scarcely a word gathered up their books, bowed their heads sadly, and were gone.

And so ended the only little day of sunlight that had broken through the clouds for a long, long time. They had been so humble, so willing to learn, so ready to help, in their helpless way, so patient, so filled with that dignity which is the only humility, and that humility which is the only perfect dignity, that he had learned to love them truly and deeply. They had had that spirit of meekness in them that could wash a brother's feet and yet not seem foolish. And when they went away he bowed his head in his hands at the table and was well-nigh broken-hearted.

But he took up the Book after a time and read once more the Sermon on the Mount. Then he read it again. He closed the lids a little bit savagely after this last reading. He spent the next few days in the canyon, cutting out the poison-oak, — a task which none other had ever been willing to perform.

How weary in spirit he was! and she had not kept her promise to come. How sore at heart, how sick of it all! He had grown gray here in a little time. The end was not far off.

"Ah, if I could only take this deep, cool canyon, with its pleasant waters and its profound woods, and go to some far-away place! But no; that would be turning my back on the battle to which God has set my face. I shall fight it out here. Happily, it will not be long now; whatever comes, I shall not run away."

The next day was Sunday. The big German came, came alone, with his coat thrown leisurely over his arm. The hermit was at his little desk in his study, as was his habit on this day.

"Ah, Mr. Morton, Japs gone, eh? That's right; plenty of good German girls to be had, and they are lots better than Japs. But I want to see you about your cutting down the shade from the water in the canyon. Of course it is on your own ground; but you see the water runs down by me. I want the water kept cool for my ducks and pigs and chickens. Now, if you cut down the bushes, that lets in the sun, that makes the water warm. My lawyer, he say if you do that you must pay me."

"How much pay do you want?"

"Vell, Mr. Morton, I will not be hard. We can agree, I think. Can you pay me a little now? That will bind the bargain, my lawyer say."

"Come over into the canyon and I will pay you there."

"Good, good! we will get on. I have always tried to help you, as you were a new settler; and now you are going to oblige me."

The man had snatched his overcoat from

the wall and was walking fast; the German ran along at his side.

The road was a road of roses; but the man walked too fast to heed the roses, or even hear the many friendly speeches which the garrulous German was making from time to time, as he came puffing on after him.

There was a big heap of stones on the high summit just before descending the steep path into the canyon. The sun was warm, hot. He threw his heavy coat against the high mound of stones under the olive-tree he had planted, and hastened on, the German at his heels.

XIII. — FALLEN BY THE WAY.

"How shall man surely save his soul?"
  'T was sunset by the Jordan. Gates
Of light were closing, and the whole
  Vast heaven hung darkened as the fates.
"How shall man surely save his soul;" he said,
As fell the kingly day, discrowned and dead.

The Christ said: "Hear this parable.
  Two men set forth and journeyed fast
To reach a place ere darkness fell
  And closed the gates ere they had passed;
Two worthy men, each free alike of sin,
But one did seek most sure to enter in.

"And so when in their path did lay
  A cripple with a broken staff,
The one did pass straight on his way,
  While one did stoop and give the half
His strength, and all his time did nobly share
Till they at sunset saw their city fair.

"And he who would make sure ran fast
  To reach the golden sunset gate,
Where captains and proud chariots passed,
  But lo, he came one moment late!
The gate was closed, and all night long he cried;
He cried and cried, but never watch replied.

"Meanwhile, the man who cared to save
  Another as he would be saved
Came slowly on, gave bread and gave
  Cool waters, and he stooped and laved
The wounds. At last, bent double with his weight,
He passed, unchid, the porter's private gate.

"Hear then this lesson, hear and learn:
He who would save his soul, I say,
Must lose his soul; must dare to turn
And lift the fallen by the way;
Must make his soul worth saving by some deed
That grows, and rows, as grows the fruitful seed."

As said before, the silent man with set lips cast aside the coat on his arm as he reached the rocky summit where he had planted the olive-tree. It had flourished wonderfully. As he hastily threw the coat beneath its beautiful green and gray and dove-colored branches and hurried on down over the high, steep brow of the hill he did not see the symbol of peace at all. His eyes were blinded with rage. He led on and on down the steep and wooded road to the very bed of the canyon.

The robust German followed close at his heels. His mind was full of speculation and expectation. He had become convinced that his neighbor, the dreamer, was entirely helpless; that his lands were surely slipping from his tired hands; that they must fall into the hands of some one, and why not as well into his hands as those of another?

"Yes, down here in the deep canyon he will make some concessions for the sake of peace, as he always does, and as there will be no witness I can fix it up to suit myself. And he, of course, will consent to whatever I say, for the sake of peace. Let me see, I must have a little money to bind the bargain; a little spot cash, if only one dollar, to bind the bargain, my lawyer say, and —"

The big man's calculations were suddenly interrupted. They had reached the dense redwood grove at the bottom of the canyon, and Morton had wheeled sharply about. His back was to the largest of the lovely little redwood-trees; and his face only a few feet from that of his robust neighbor.

The peaceful brook purled and rattled along in its bed of rocks and pebbles, birds sang pleasantly from the further hillside in the sun, but all else was silent. The place was as secure from intrusion as a country churchyard.

The man drew in his breath sharp and quick and said hastily, between his teeth:

"You are well to-day?"

"Yes, yes, never so vell; but I am varm. I puts on my coat, so I vill not take cold."

"No! you will not take cold. You will not have time to take cold!"

"Why, what do you mean?"

"What do I mean? I told you I would

pay you, settle with you, here in the canyon, and I intend to keep my word."

The German was not dull; neither was he a coward. He saw that there was battle in the eye of his outraged neighbor, and in a second he threw his coat aside and prepared to meet it like a man.

With right foot forward and his big, red fists in rest, he awaited the onset. But his neighbor was not now in such great haste. There was a pause, and the German, who really knew himself all along to have been terribly in the wrong, took quick occasion to say, "Is this your Sermon on the Mount?"

"Yes, yes, it is. For I have read it over and over since I read it to you, and I find it is written there that you shall not give that which is holy unto *dogs*, nor cast pearls before *swine*."

It was too much, that peculiarly personal accent given the allusion to the low creatures named; and the German, suddenly blinded with rage, struck out terribly with his big, red, right fist.

He was a huge man, nearly twice the weight of his neighbor and not so old. But he had not spent the past five years in wrestling with the elements on a mountain side. His had been a sedentary life in the city;

and so his first blow, which spent its force above the mark, as he stood on ground higher than that of his sinewy opponent, was his last. But he forced the fighting like a good German soldier as he was, and bore down heavily on the man, who stood with his back to the tree, and at last, by sheer weight and force, he bore him to the ground.

But, as in the story of old, the earth came to the rescue. The dear old mother earth, whom he had loved and on whose bosom he had rested, or wrought in forms of beauty for years past, came to his help as she came to the help of the shepherd king of old. He sprang to his feet with renewed life. The German again stood before him, formidable indeed to look upon, but almost breathless.

Bang! bang! bang! The first landed with terrific force on the big man's big throat. His head was thrown back by the blow, and before he could recover the first was followed by the second, and the second by the third on the same unguarded column.

The big, red fists fell to the big man's side. The big mouth opened and the big man gasped helplessly, but could not even find breath to cry out for mercy. The battle was over.

"Come now and be washed; then go and

tell your Dutch and Irish friends that it was poison-oak. What! Do you want more? Come! and be decent about it, or I'll thresh you till you do."

The big man had held back as disdaining to accept help from his enemy; but the other man would not be trifled with now,— the rage of battle was on him; and so, accepting the outreaching hand of help, he suffered himself to be led down to the pretty little brook, over which he bowed his big head, gasping and gasping for breath, and was washed as if he had been a new-born babe.

Pretty soon he stood erect, then he stooped over, washed his face with his own hands and then rose up and slowly wiped his face and his hands with his handkerchief.

At last, lifting his head, he looked his neighbor full in the face as he reached his right hand. The other took it and shook it heartily.

"Dot's all right; you cuts down vot you likes."

With this the German gathered up his coat and took his way down the canyon toward his home.

The city-builder looked after him, his heart bursting with shame and humiliation. He wanted to run after him, to bring him back, to beg his pardon, to beg his pardon on his knees. But the chill and damp of twilight soon began to creep into his bones, and he slowly ascended to the olive-tree on the high hilltop where he had thrown aside his coat. He gathered the garment about his chilled shoulders, and too weary to go further, he lay with his face to the dust. He had never been so entirely miserable in all his miserable life.

How continually he had taught all men the wisdom, the duty, the beauty of turning the other cheek! and yet, here he had gone down to the low and bestial level of a poor ignorant foreigner and fought and fought as a dog might fight.

True, he had been tempted, terribly tempted; but he had fallen so low, so foolishly, that he could now no longer hold up his head or have the heart to go forward with his lessons of love and beauty and duty at all.

He lay there on his face, and he felt that surely the end of all his hopes and aspirations had come.

In his despair his thoughts kept continually turning to her, Miriam. Where was she? What had he done that she had not kept her promise? Five years had swept by.

He had missed her presence, her calm counsel, serene wisdom, so much all the time; and as hope began to falter, and all things to fall away from him, he had come to think of her continually and to wish for her or death. "I will come to you — sometime." And now that he needed her so entirely his soul went out to her entirely, — a poor, lone dove on the deluge of waters, that found no place for the sole of its foot.

He lay there on the heights in the gathering night, and, as his heart went out to her, he continually repeated, " I will come to you — sometime;" and then he murmured, "Lead us not into temptation! Lead us not into temptation!"

XIV. — UNDER THE OLIVE-TREES.

Those shining leaves that lisped and shook
  All darkness from them, sensate leaves
In Nature's never-ending book;
  Leaves full of truth as garnered sheaves
That hold till seed-time fruitful seed,
To grow as grows some small good deed.

How strangely and how vastly still!
  The harvest moon hung low and large,
And drew across the dreamful hill
  Like some huge star-bound, freighted barge;
Some strange, new, neighbor-world it surely seemed,
The while he gazed and dreamed, yet scarcely dreamed.

THE poor, discouraged dreamer under the little olive-tree on the high peak above the sea was so very sore in soul, and so very sore in body too! He could have borne with the last; but the two together made him earnestly wish to die and leave it all with the one word "Failure" for his epitaph.

After a time the ever-welcome winds, warm and balmy as with a healing balm, blew in and on and away down toward the Mexican seas from Japan.

"'Oh that I had the wings of the dove, to fly away and be at rest!'" he sighed piteously, as the warm, strong winds went on by,

He had missed her presence, her calm counsel, serene wisdom, so much all the time; and as hope began to falter, and all things to fall away from him, he had come to think of her continually and to wish for her or death. "I will come to you — sometime." And now that he needed her so entirely his soul went out to her entirely, — a poor, lone dove on the deluge of waters, that found no place for the sole of its foot.

He lay there on the heights in the gathering night, and, as his heart went out to her, he continually repeated, "I will come to you — sometime;" and then he murmured, "Lead us not into temptation! Lead us not into temptation!"

XIV. — UNDER THE OLIVE-TREES.

Those shining leaves that lisped and shook
   All darkness from them, sensate leaves
In Nature's never-ending book;
   Leaves full of truth as garnered sheaves
That hold till seed-time fruitful seed,
To grow as grows some small good deed.

How strangely and how vastly still!
   The harvest moon hung low and large,
And drew across the dreamful hill
   Like some huge star-bound, freighted barge;
Some strange, new, neighbor-world it surely seemed,
The while he gazed and dreamed, yet scarcely dreamed.

THE poor, discouraged dreamer under the little olive-tree on the high peak above the sea was so very sore in soul, and so very sore in body too! He could have borne with the last; but the two together made him earnestly wish to die and leave it all with the one word "Failure" for his epitaph.

After a time the ever-welcome winds, warm and balmy as with a healing balm, blew in and on and away down toward the Mexican seas from Japan.

"'Oh that I had the wings of the dove, to fly away and be at rest!'" he sighed piteously, as the warm, strong winds went on by, bearing their snow-white fleets and happy voyagers. Surely, these clouds that drove by below, about, above, were mighty ships that bore sweet souls bound heavenward.

From the city and the mountain-side below him came up the song and the melody of the closing day. Still further below, many and many a church spire pierced the warm, white clouds that blew in from the sea and drew softly through the tree-tops above the city. The sound of church bells came up to him through the world of clouds; came up to him there under the little olive-tree, as if they had lost their way, as he had lost his way, there on the stony steeps of his mountain.

Beyond all this the bosom of the great bay of San Francisco rose and fell with the sea of seas, and gleamed and glistened and gloried in the face of God as if a living thing.

At the Golden Gate, without, the great sea, with its hundred thousand white-clad choristers, sang and sang and sang.

A huge sea-lion from the seal rocks beyond the city of San Francisco rose out of the sea, climbed to the top of the crags, and there lifted his bearded face straight up in the air, and mouthed and mouthed his doleful monotone till it rolled and rose above the clang of the church bells and above the songs of the hundred thousand white-clad singers of the sea of seas.

And still the soft and balmy winds came in continually with their warmth and healing from the dreamful seas of Japan.

But the man under the olive-tree was miserable, utterly miserable, for all this melody, all this harmony of sea and song, this harmony of heaven and earth.

"Oh, why may I not build a ship of clouds and launch it on this strong, sweet current that flows in so steadily from Japan? Surely, surely science might make a ship to sail these mighty streams of the upper world! Why, men have been sailing their helpless little air-ships in the valley, from little town towers for centuries; but who has dared these brave, big currents that keep place in heaven like mighty rivers which turn not to the right nor left, but keep straight on? Surely, when the great navigator comes he will launch his stately ships upon these strong and steady currents. Man has kept his face to the ground in quest of gold; but some day, some great and good and really wise Columbus will come, and will launch his ships here on these strong, swift, sweet currents of Japan, and sail to the undiscovered continents of heaven."

Such were the weary and desolate man's dreamful and confused thoughts as he lay there wrapped in the large solemnity of gathering night. Meantime, the countless belts and curves and crescents of electric lights leaped suddenly into existence and climbed to the top of mountains beyond the city of San Francisco. The stars had stood there but a moment before. Now, one could not tell where the lights left off or the stars began.

The gorgeous and flaming star of Mars had hung just above the grand and indescribably pathetic figure of "Our Mother of Pain," at whose feet the pious and patient men of God, a full century before, had built their holy little temple, the Mission Dolores.

The strangely brilliant battle-star was settling down, down, down, straight between the lifted breasts of the Holy Virgin where they lift perpetually, as in the piteous agonies of motherhood.

The man's racked and wearied senses wandered now, and grew confused with the sea of lights in which his star lay drowning at the feet of Our Mother of Sorrows. For now the face and figure of the most divinely glorious being ever seen seemed to be dimly limned out before him; and the Star of

Bethlehem was in her wondrous night of hair. It was she, Miriam, that wondrous woman of Jerusalem and of Egypt. "I will come to you — sometime." She had come.

And a ship was there! Was it but a cloud? Surely there was no mistaking the fact of the strong and steady stream from Japan.

It seemed to him that no word had been said as he arose from under the olive-tree, entered the ship, and so sailed on and on and on. They sailed by the porch of heaven. It was pavilioned with stars, propped by awful arches formed of uncompleted worlds.

They sailed beneath the Milky Way, that seemed as some great arch above a surging river. They sailed above the clouds, above the sinking moon, above all storms and counterstorms; and the mighty river which, like the Gulf Stream, girdled the world, swept on and on and on.

Black and white and storm-tossed clouds were banked below or heaped on either side. These seas and shores of tumbled clouds were bed and banks of this awful Gulf Stream of the upper world, on whose strong and certain currents the air-ship sailed and sailed and sailed.

It was full morning when he landed; and he was alone. The ship had rested on a pine-set mountain-top. A vast valley lay below. In the centre of this valley, sand-sown and tawny as a desert of Africa all about its borders, lay gleaming like silver in the morning sun a city of indescribable splendor and magnitude.

Almost overcome with awe and wonder, the man descended from the car, keeping his eyes fixed on the far-off city amid its groves in the heart of the tawny desert.

Descending through the pines a little distance down a well-worn road, he came to a small station. A man approached him, but he kept turning about to look for the silent and serenely beautiful Madonna, who had accompanied him in the glorious voyage above the world. He saw her not, and was sad.

Olive-trees, orange-trees, birds, bees, blossoms — a railroad depot in the midst of all this, and yet all things so like one perpetual Sunday. It was as quiet, as restful, as flowery here as the entrance of some gorgeous church on some Easter Sunday, — as if the people were waiting for the minister to come in. Yes, there was the music, and such music! No shrieking, soul-tearing sounds — sounds in combat, notes in battle, notes at war with notes — such as distract the civilized (?) earth from end to end; no sickening smells and other abominations that hold high carnival at the average depot in the outer world.

Peace, peace, peace! Melody, poetry, Paradise!

And yet, this was surely all on the solid earth; for the man who came forward and touched his cap to the stranger was gray about the temples. Surely he, at least, had not yet done with time. People were coming and people were going, just as elsewhere; old people and young people, plain and beautiful.

"The train starts exactly on the hour. You see that you have time to take your seat for the city."

A hand indicated a high tower where a great clock hung above the few, brief rules, the set times for coming and going.

As the stranger took his seat he could not help missing those ever-present lies that are set up in any depot on earth: "Shortest route!" "Only safe line!" "Quickest and cheapest line to the city."

In fact, as he looked out through the car, — for the cars were made of malleable glass, transparent as air and indestructible as brass (one of the lost arts restored), — he could not but note the entire absence of the decorative advertisement.

The shapely clock-tower, with its girdles of brass and its sides of broad bronze, was a goodly place for "posters," too.

But these unenterprising people had not even put up a sign to say that space on this tower for advertising purposes was to be had cheaper than on any other clock-tower on the road.

Without a word or sound or sign from any one save from the clock in the tower and the little clocks at the end of each car that indicated not only the time but the name of each station, they glided out and they glided on.

Inquiring of a pleasant-faced priest at his side, he learned, to his great relief — for he had neither scrip nor purse — that as the roads all belonged to the people, the people did not take tribute of themselves nor of the stranger within their gates who came to honor them with his presence.

"I have surely been here before," said the man at last, as if to himself, while he sat looking out upon the beautiful groves and roads of roses and bananas and wooded parks through which the swift and silent cars continually descended.

"If you will allow me," began the kindly monk, "that is a matter, the idea of having been here before, which we have under deep consideration."

"Will you explain?"

"Certainly. Meditative people are almost constantly seeing something in this life that they say they have surely seen before; and that something is always something beautiful or grand or inspiring, appealing to the best that is in us. And this, some of us, at least, take to be one of the tangible and visible evidences of immortality. This, some of us hold to be pretty clear evidence that we not only shall live hereafter, but that we have lived long, long before. No, no, my son, you have never looked on this scene in this life, previous to this; for it is all very new. But it may be that somewhere else, in some other world, or at least in some other life, you, in a happy moment of harmony with all things, saw something very like this, under restful and harmonious conditions very like to these," said the priest, thoughtfully.

The stranger was dumb with wonder and delight. He had at last and for the first time since leaving the lady of Jerusalem by the Nile come into an atmosphere of thought in which his soul if not his body had been born from the first. He lifted his hat and sat uncovered in silence. Cottages, fields of corn, cane, cotton, a lane of banana-trees shut out the sun from the gliding palaces of glass all along now.

"And all this, you tell me, was only an arid sea of gleaming sand and baked mud a few years ago?"

"Certainly; we at first found rain hard to produce; but we had been prudent enough to bring with us something better than the natural storms of rain, — intelligence, and a colony of scientific men and women. We now have rain whenever it is needed, but never when it is not needed."

"Indeed! And such cars!"

"Yes," said the priest, "we make glass houses, railway ties, railway tracks, and railway cars, as you see here."

"And they never break?"

"Glass is not only elastic, as all know, but glass, by our redemption of a lost art, is made as malleable as gold or copper."

It is hardly known what more the priest said or might have said, as they glided on down under the great banana-trees; for just then the stranger caught a glimpse of a party gathering bananas. They were girls, up in the trees among the birds, buried in the broad leaves, an arm thrusting up after the yellow fruit, a brown limb thrusting out below, drawn back, bound around and twined about a branch to hold fast! Ah! he forgot that a priest was within a thousand miles of him.

Many stations, many short stops, then on and on through the continuous and seemingly endless lane of laden trees.

At one of the little, leafy stations the priest put forth his hand and received from a pretty Indian girl two yellow bananas. They were like yellow ears of corn, so large were they. And such flavor!

"The world, the outside commercial world," said the priest as he handed one to the stranger, "has never yet tasted a banana. Those wild things, gathered green by savages of the Cannibal Islands and thrown into the holds of sailing vessels to rot and ripen, ripen and rot, are not bananas. They are disease. They are death, death for little children, old people, young people, all people."

At last they glided over a glass bridge that spanned a bent lagoon. The central railway station, where they now stopped and from which all tracks, trains, pneumatic tubes, airship-lines, and even streets and highways ran, was simply a palace, a glorious palace of glass, blue above as the sky is blue; and under foot the solid earth, snow-white sand, with fountains bursting up through, blossoming trees, and birds in every tree, and a song in the throat of every bird; for all things were so beautiful and all things were so happy the birds could but sing.

XV. — AS WHEN THE CHRIST SHALL COME AGAIN.

From out the golden doors of dawn
   The wise men came, of wondrous thought,
Who knew the stars. From far upon
   The shoreless East they kneeling brought
Their costly gifts of inwrought gems and gold,
While cloudlike incense from their presence rolled.

Their sweets of flower fields, their sweet
   Distilments of most sacred leaves
They laid, low-bending, at His feet,
   As reapers bend above their sheaves —
As strong-armed reapers bending clamorous
To gather golden full sheaves kneeling thus.

And kneeling so, they spake of when
   God walked His garden's sacred sod,
Nor yet had hid His face from men,
   Nor yet had man forgotten God.
They spake. But Mary kept her thought apart
And, silent, "pondered all things in her heart."

They spake in whispers long, they laid
   Their shaggy heads together, drew
Some stained scrolls breathless forth, then made
   Such speech as only wise men knew, — '
Their high, red camels on the huge hill set
Outstanding, like some night-hewn silhouette.

THE stranger was hungry, — more than hungry, he was famishing. The good priest knew this, — knew it not from words, maybe not from look, act, or utterance. But so sensitive and refined had these people grown here, even in a few years of meditation and unselfishness, that they really knew the thoughts and feelings of one another, — as horses, dogs and other lower animals know our desires and designs. More of this, however, later on.

Over and across a wide, snow-white, sand-sown avenue of banana-trees, where no cart, car, carriage, or any other rumbling nuisance could pass, the good priest led to a public restaurant by a great fountain.

"Not being a strong man," he began as they sat down, "I chose the duties of a waiter when I came, and I serve my two hours of daily toil here. However, my toil, I regret to say, must come to an end next year, as I shall then be sixty. This man who will wait on us now is a young Methodist clergyman, or rather he was a Methodist clergyman. But as all roads run in together as we approach any one city or centre of any sort, so here, as we attain peace and approach something nearer the common centre of more perfect life, we find all religions running in together. We are all walking along so nearly together here, in fact, that we can and do touch hands across the narrow and dim little lines that divide us."

"Well, well, well! and you say you, a not very strong man, will lay aside the menial employment of a common servant, or waiter, at the age of sixty, with regret?"

"Certainly. I really and truly like to serve. If Christ could wash his disciples' feet, might I not give bread to a hungry man; or even wash a hungry man's plate?"

The stranger held his peace a moment, and then, as the choice repast was served, ate in silent amazement as the priest continued:—

"But of course I cannot be idle. After reaching sixty years I must begin to hold office; so I shall be required to serve the Republic many years still, if I live. In fact, no man or woman who lives long enough can hardly escape serving a term as president."

"May I be permitted to know the mystery of it all?"

"There is no mystery at all. Mystery there may be in other republics, where presidents, and often thousands of other officers are chosen by man's popular voice, but not so here. God, Nature, elects our every officer. You see, any one coming here from the outer world, and all who are born here are registered,— age, occupation, and so on. Well, every one attaining the age of seventy becomes a senator, and the oldest persons in the Senate comprise the Council. The oldest of these is president, and is usually a person of eighty; for we live in the full enjoyment of all our faculties at least ten years longer than in the outside world, where the brain and body are strained and strung till they break from the very tension."

"And then you have no elections at all?"

"Yes, the election of nature; the choice of God."

The stranger shook his head at this intensely democratic proposition.

"I see you do not entirely approve of leaving the election to God. You fear that some bad or foolish man may by this means attain the head of government. Listen to me. Does not the Declaration of Independence of a certain great nation assert that 'all men are born free and equal'? Now, if we are born equal how is it that we become so unequal as we go forward in the great outer world? Why, you see some are hit, hit hard in the hot and bitter battle of life. Wrong, insult, oppression, hard work, hunger, — ay, hunger, hunger of body and soul, — these things dwarf, break down the very best and finest of you. And so it is that you in the outer world, with your lawyers, your politicians, your idle parsons and your idle priests, your lying money-lenders and land-agents, your oppressive middle men, eleven idle and scheming men to the one slave at work, one man working ten, fifteen, twenty hours, if he can stand up under it— Ah me! no wonder that man succeeds, with all this evil and ill-doing, in making unequal that which God has made equal."

They had risen and passed out into the street. The stranger was full of wonder, and entirely silent with awe and admiration. And yet he could not help recalling the fact that he had somewhere, far back in life, heard much of this which was being uttered here. His mind went back to a voyage up the Nile, to a night amid the ruins of fearful Karnak, to the glory and the serene beauty of a dark and splendid face there. His soul went out continually to the grand and silent woman who had come to him in the clouds only the night before and had carried him away and out of his world of cares, out of himself, to this, her world.

"You are thinking of her?"

"Of whom?"

"Well, no matter about her name. Let us say our guardian angel. I am desirous of leading you to her. Shall we proceed directly to her, or wait till to-morrow? To-morrow were better."

"At once, please God, at once!" cried the man, with clasped hands, as he saw the kindly man hesitate.

"You need rest."

"Indeed, indeed, I do not need rest. I am strong as a lion. I need only her — to see her."

A shade of concern and deep sadness swept over the sensitive priest's face, as if he had something in his mind which he hesitated to tell. At last he said: —

"Yes, yes, you are strong."

"And she — she, my Madonna, Miriam — she is not strong?"

"Far, far from strong, my son."

The priest's head was on his breast as he spoke. Then lifting his face he said pleasantly: —

"But she forbids all sadness on this score, and so I must obey her and be cheerful."

"But I may see her to-night?"

"To-morrow, my son, to-morrow."

XVI.

> The sun lay molten in the sea
> Of sand, and all the sea was rolled
> In one broad, bright intensity
> Of gold and gold and gold and gold.

As the rosy fingers of morning reached out of heaven, laid aside night's sombre mantle from the mountain-tops and lightly touched the tawny bosom of the desert, a vision of indescribable splendor rose up from the far-off levels of boundless yellow sands to the east.

Golden sunlight and glittering yellow sands were warp and woof, and all woven into one. You could not say which was sunlight and which was sea, which was gold or golden sun.

But the miracle of it all was the forest of spires, minarets, towers, pyramids, obelisks and the like that rose, a mirage, above the levels of the desert. The cross, the crescent, the fire-worshipper's glowing signs of the rising sun, all were here in amazing magnitude; and all in gorgeous glory and harmony of form and color.

Far away they seemed, like the dim and distant outlines of some glorious New Jerusalem, or an inspired dream of a prophet of God.

"Beautiful! Beautiful! Beautiful! Oh, that is indeed my dream of the City Beautiful! Would to God it could be real!" sighed the man as he turned away his eyes a moment to rest them from the splendid sight.

"It is all real," said the priest, gently. He had come in with the sun to see what he might do to serve the stranger; for here there was no occasion for locks or closed doors, for clerks or call-boys.

"All real? That, that all real? Then you found the City of the Sun on coming to this wilderness. You surely found one of the fabled cities of gold that the daring Spaniard searched for so persistently," said the man, as he turned again and looked upon the glorious spectacle.

"No, we built it all. We still are building; for our work is only begun."

The man threw out his hand and caught the priest desperately by the arm.

"Let me go back to the hard realities of my rocks, for I shall go mad if I see more of these splendid visions, and then after all have to waken and see them fade to nothing."

The priest sat down beside him, holding

him tenderly by the hand which had been thrown out so wildly toward him.

"I assert it is all real," he said. "You see, at first, when we came and settled here where the old Toltec ruins lay, we had not progressed in science so far as we now have. Then our learned men had not emancipated themselves, and so were busy breaking the shackles; and then it took time to experiment and give full play and practice to their designs. But now they can build a city in the desert almost in a day."

The stranger looked at the priest a moment hard and steadily. A gentle and reassuring pressure of the hand was his only answer. Finally the priest said: —

"If you will look toward the right of the loftiest obelisk you will see a most stately pyramid. That is the first thing built by their new process, as a sort of experiment."

The man looked, and beheld what seemed to him a pyramid more noble than that of Cheops. The priest went on.

"Of course there was nothing new in this building a pyramid out of desert sands. This was rather an acknowledgment to the Egyptians. They claim only to have restored a lost art."

"How, what?"

The man had hastily pressed the fingers of his left hand hard against his burning forehead; for a strange and sudden thought had pierced his brain. The priest continued:

"There must have been great inundations of sand from Sahara in the olden time. And this sand had to be disposed of. They could not continually pour it into the Nile, and so they cemented it and built the pyramids out of it, — yes, carried it up on their backs, perhaps, and there fused and cemented and melted it into shapely blocks as they desired by the use of chemicals. And so they got rid of the sand and had the shapely pyramids to look upon and perpetuate the story of the lost arts of immortal and glorious old Egypt."

By this time the man had laid his left hand on the hand of the priest which held his own. But he was too eager to listen, and to learn, to do more than this, or to even move his lips.

"But," continued the priest with enthusiasm, "our scientists have done more than restore this lost art in the building of cities. There are no beasts of burthen here as in Egypt. In freedom, where men can really follow their natural and wholesome desires, labor is free to choose its vocation and its hours. Necessity does not force a man to do the most menial work. The hardest toiler gets the best pay with us, and the pleasantest tasks the lightest pay. This naturally leads to the employment of science to make labor's tasks light and pleasant, rather than merely profitable to the employer. I spoke of the fusing of sand with chemicals. Well, now, an elevator is not a pretty thing, nor a poetical thing, nor is it quite what I mean; but if you keep in your mind the idea of an elevator, such as is used in the loading of wheat, you will have an idea of the way in which we gather up sand from the desert and carry it to the top of our tallest edifices, and then melt it into column and spire and dome, as readily and easily as you can write your name in the sand with a walking-stick."

The man turned his face once more to look at tower and tomb, minaret, cross, crescent, and all the numberless works before him under the glowing sun, in the buildings of the City Beautiful. With grateful heart he cried: —

"'And the desert shall blossom as the rose.'"

"The desert," said the priest, "is the place for the rose. The only real place for the rose is in the fervid sands of the desert.

Warm sands above, artesian water below, and you have such roses as the world has not seen since the Garden of Eden. As for cities, we simply could not build, never could have built, as we have built, but for this beautiful sea of desert sand."

"I observe that you have the symbols of all religions," said the man, meditatively, after looking once more far out and under the newly risen sun.

"No, we have but one religion."

"Then why do I see all these various symbols?"

"These are but harmonies and traditions, histories in the air."

"Then what is this one religion, pray?"

The priest was silent for a long time, still holding to both the hands that had been thrust with eager inquiry into his. At last he said:—

"I should like to coin a new word. I should like to find some fusing and melting chemical, such as they use out yonder in melting and fusing together the sands in building temples and shrines in all religions. But I am not cunning in speech. Let me say, then, that our one religion is to love truth, to love country, to do good."

"And what, then, do you worship?"

Again the good priest was a long time silent. He looked down to the floor and then up and out and far away. At last he said slowly, humbly, and hardly above his breath : —

"We worship Truth, Duty, Beauty. Blend these three, this trinity and all religions together, as they blend yonder sands, and then call it God. We worship that — GOD."

XVII.—IN HER PRESENCE AT LAST.

He walked the world with bended head.
"There is no thing," he moaning said,
"That must not some day join the dead."

He sat where rolled a river deep;
A woman sat her down to weep;
A child lay in her lap asleep.

The water touched the mother's hand.
His heart was touched. He passed from land,
But left it laughing in the sand.

That one kind word, that one good deed,
Was as if you should plant a seed
In sand along death's sable brede.

And looking from the farther shore
He saw, where he had sat before,
A light that grew, grew more and more.

He saw a growing, glowing throng
Of happy people white and strong
With faith, and jubilant with song.

It grew and grew, this little seed
Of good sown in that day of need,
Until it touched the stars indeed!

And then the old man smiling said,
With youthful heart and lifted head,
"No good deed ever joins the dead."

"THE world is too much with us." We must turn back to some of the old beliefs.

We can't get to heaven on a railroad car, no matter how fast it runs. O my preachers, this railroad levelling of all things is terrible, monstrous; for it is making monsters of men, levelling them down so that their roads can cross over all religion into heaven You have explained away the parable of the rich man down in hell.

My friend, who was this Jesus Christ? There was but one Christ, a poor carpenter, who said, "Sell all that thou hast and distribute unto the poor, and come, follow me." But you are preaching another Christ entirely.

Several times Spain arose and turned out the priests who had got hold of the gold. I implore you, teach the true Christ. Tell your splendid paymasters that the people can rise up as easily as of old and turn the rich people out, as the rich priests were turned out. They can even go out, out in the wilderness as the Jews went out, and build new worlds, if their taskmasters continue to oppress them.

. . . .

As the priest and the stranger approached her wide-open door under the banana-trees, she came forward to meet them.

The same ardent sincerity, the same eloquence of silence on her pale and passionless lips! Ah, how pale she was! Her once black hair had whitened with her beautiful face. The care, toil, endurance of other days had taxed her terribly. She was now paying that tax with her precious life. And yet, she was so beautiful still! But it was the beauty of the grand old battlements of Rome in the moonlight, the majestic and mighty ruin of Karnak on the Nile at night.

Her great pathetic eyes looked at the stranger as if looking out from another world for a moment, and then she threw her two hands out as if throwing them across the years that had rolled between them. The years were spanned, swept aside, and the two were as of old.

The priest went on his way without words. There are times, and they are very frequent, when words are an impertinence.

People here, as in other parts of the semi-tropics, did not live in houses much. Without a word she slowly led out and along by the fountains and trees where the birds sang.

There were no servants, indeed no noise or friction of any sort anywhere. It seemed as though he had at last found a land on earth that had some sense of heaven. Here it seemed as if it were one eternal Sabbath. And right and left, up and down the long wooded and watered streets, people were coming and people were going; pausing now to speak to one another in a soft and restful fashion, lingering to listen, turning about to catch a last look or word, but that was all; there was no haste, and the chattering was all left to the birds.

Passing on and up and around through lanes of perfumed woods, by sparkling fountains and pleasant porches, they came to the summit, or, rather, the centre, where the great trout pools bubbled and boiled up through the massive blocks and broken ruins of some pre-historic Toltec city. She paused here to rest a moment, and turned to look below. She put out her hand. He comprehended her thought.

She had indeed built a city, her City Beautiful in the desert. This, where they stood, was the hub of a wheel; in every direction ran the spokes; at the tips of the spokes and far out and around at the foot of the mountains ran a track of glass, around which cars of glass kept gliding, as spiders glide along, around and over their own little world of curious and intricate web, in silence and harmonious perfection.

"But the title-deeds to it all? The world will come this way some day, and then—"

"Ah, that I have provided for. You are a dreamer, I am a builder. You are of heaven, but I am only of earth. I searched Mexico City through and found that the owner of this desert lived there; and I bought the whole fifty leagues of desert for a small sum. And so you see I have in this, at least, lived up to the Lord's Prayer: 'Lead us not into temptation;' for no man will be tempted to try to take this land from us. I, in turn, have given all, by irrevocable will, to our people. There is not a human being here, from the priest who brought you here to the babe born within this hour, who is not a full partner in all the real interests of this city of the desert. We have no disinherited. The coming together of my people does not enrich some without toil. The landless do not pay tribute to the landlords. All are equal owners in natural and social values.

"The curse of all society is the granting of special privileges which are the survivals of the divine right of force and fraud. I determined that my city should exist for the granting and preserving of equal rights. I determined that there should be no privileges granted to the few. We have no monopoly laws; we have no patent-rights, or copyrights, even."

"But is that just?" said the man. "Has not a man a right to his book?"

"He has a right to sell his book once, but not for a half-century. It is just, when all privileges are abolished together. Then each man invents for all and all the rest invent for him. It is a free exchange of benefits."

The man's face shone. "I see!" he said. "The incentive to invention is the love of it; the reward is the pleasure of creating."

She arose and they walked on, his mind exalted with the new idea.

"And they are all so happy and prosperous!" he exclaimed, his mind turning back to the brown girls he had seen gathering fruit among the broad leaves as he glided down from the mountain the day before.

"So happy, so healthy, and so beautiful," she continued, as they entered a retreat where she threw herself on a lion's skin that covered a broad silken couch. He sank at her side. He put out his hand to touch and take hers to his heart. She did not repel him. She did not take her hand away. She did not disdain his touch; but somehow her

"But the title-deeds to it all? The world will come this way some day, and then—"

"Ah, that I have provided for. You are a dreamer, I am a builder. You are of heaven, but I am only of earth. I searched Mexico City through and found that the owner of this desert lived there; and I bought the whole fifty leagues of desert for a small sum. And so you see I have in this, at least, lived up to the Lord's Prayer: 'Lead us not into temptation;' for no man will be tempted to try to take this land from us. I, in turn, have given all, by irrevocable will, to our people. There is not a human being here, from the priest who brought you here to the babe born within this hour, who is not a full partner in all the real interests of this city of the desert. We have no disinherited. The coming together of my people does not enrich some without toil. The landless do not pay tribute to the landlords. All are equal owners in natural and social values.

"The curse of all society is the granting of special privileges which are the survivals of the divine right of force and fraud. I determined that my city should exist for the granting and preserving of equal rights. I determined that there should be no privileges granted to the few. We have no monopoly laws; we have no patent-rights, or copyrights, even."

"But is that just?" said the man. "Has not a man a right to his book?"

"He has a right to sell his book once, but not for a half-century. It is just, when all privileges are abolished together. Then each man invents for all and all the rest invent for him. It is a free exchange of benefits."

The man's face shone. "I see!" he said. "The incentive to invention is the love of it; the reward is the pleasure of creating."

She arose and they walked on, his mind exalted with the new idea.

"And they are all so happy and prosperous!" he exclaimed, his mind turning back to the brown girls he had seen gathering fruit among the broad leaves as he glided down from the mountain the day before.

"So happy, so healthy, and so beautiful," she continued, as they entered a retreat where she threw herself on a lion's skin that covered a broad silken couch. He sank at her side. He put out his hand to touch and take hers to his heart. She did not repel him. She did not take her hand away. She did not disdain his touch; but somehow her soul seemed far, far away, above him, so far above him. So much larger she seemed as he sat there in his narrow vanity and selfishness, that he felt like crouching down in the dust at her feet.

How tranquilly grand she was in all her silent splendor. Time had only made her more glorious, glorious in body as in soul it seemed now, now as she sat there all aglow and flushed with the excitement of their meeting. But it was only momentary with her, this flush and glow and glory of form and face. Beauty there was, and glow and color, fervor and fire even; but it was the fire and glow of the dying sun.

The kindly old priest came back after a time to take the stranger with him. They wandered away together, and in a quiet way he talked very earnestly of himself to the stranger, and as nearly as can be recalled as follows: —

"As for being a priest, I am a priest; and yet I am not now all priest. It did not seem good to me that the people should be ignorant and dependent to the end of time. If the world is to lay aside the sword and turn to the ploughshare it must be done intelligently if done permanently. Love must be in the hearts of the people as well as in the hearts of the priests. Religion must be a fact, not merely a form. The people are good, the world is beautiful, and God is love. Let the child that comes laughing down out of heaven to us, clapping its tiny hands with delight all day in the open fields, not be told that it is sinful, and that the world is wicked, and that God is angry with this beautiful world which he has made for man. No, no! God has made each child happy, and it should be forbidden that man, priest or layman, should make it unhappy. What evangelist has ever yet gone forth preaching faith in man? Not one. But man is and ever has been preaching the depravity of man. Man seems even to try to show the goodness of God by publishing his own wickedness. It is high time to stop this. You cannot make even a child good by forever forcing it to believe it is bad.

"Let man go into the desert, having faith in God as Moses had, but above all faith in man; and with the gospel of peace and good will he can, in this age, when savage men and savage beasts have ceased to be, build such a New Jerusalem as the world has never dreamed of.

"Look at Salt Lake, — ignorant leaders, a degrading religion, the lowest of Europe for a following, one tenth to the church, much time and hard toil to the temple; and yet the Union to-day contains no better, happier, or more prosperous people. Therefore preach that man is good, open the sea doors and let hungry Europe come to people our deserts."

The City Builder found himself being irresistibly drawn toward this thoughtful man. He asked him to tell how it was that he came to walk out and down from his high place and take up his home in the desert.

Very deliberately he began, after some reflection, and spoke, as nearly as can be recalled, to this effect: —

"There is a sort of Free Masonry, as it were, among men in the world of thought; a sort of common ground, common sense, in upper worlds of thought. The eminent theologian is not necessarily a more religious man than the eminent mathematician. The eminent mathematician is not of necessity a wiser man than the eminent theologian. But in this age of advancement all thinkers of all creeds or callings have a community of thought on the common ground of commonsense. And looking out and down from this, oftentimes with their gray heads laid close together, they have had their hearts torn continually at the contemplation of the misery of men. The eminent and thoughtful theologians, most especially, have deplored and continue to deplore this misery, so inseparably interwoven, in the present order of things, with falsehood practised in the name of Jesus Christ. Now, of these eminent men of the church there are, and long have been, two distinct kinds: one the kind that pities the misery and deplores the ignorance and deceit, but at the same time sees no way out of it all, and believes that the misery and the ignorance and the deceit are inseparable, and that the best thing to do is to leave things as they are and go right along with all the falsehoods and all the forms and all the fees. The other kind of man among the eminent theologians is one who desires to despise forms and ceremonies and shams, and to walk in the footprints of the meek and lowly Nazarene, without pay or price. Of course there is a third class, or kind of theologian, so-called, and this is, by far the most numerous. But remember, I have been speaking of eminent men, of thinkers, not of men who enter the church as they enter the army, merely for the money and to escape that one first command of God when man was driven out of Eden, which was, 'In the sweat of thy face shalt thou eat bread.' But as this large class weighs nothing in the world of thought, I need not speak of it again. The second kind referred to, however, is more numerous than one would at first believe. So, when I learned that an attempt was to be made somewhere in the deserts of America to found a community as an example to the world, on the plain brief precepts, principles, example, and sermons of Jesus Christ, I turned my back on forms and begged to be of it. And then I wanted to help destroy gold and silver, the root of so much evil; and having long had a theory that gold and silver grow, as mosses or even as potatoes grow, I wanted time and room and place to put it to the test."

"And it is you, you who made all this gold and silver that glitters everywhere in such profusion? So much gold, and yet a waiter!"

"A waiter has simply combined some of God's elements and put them in favorable place to grow. The potato which Magellan found in Brazil was not fit to eat. Now it feeds half the world; and I can pave the whole world with gold."

"But," exclaimed the startled stranger,

"this discovery will upset the whole commercial world."

"There is a God," answered his companion, gravely; "and this discovery, like the discovery of America, like the discovery of the properties of steam, electricity, all great and good things, came in its full season. The pursuit of wealth, like the ancient pursuit of war, has had its uses as well as its abuses. The world in its swift progress is fast leaving the latter far behind, — though there are still those who think the butchery of their brothers a noble pursuit and a fair expression of that law of nature which insists on the survival of the fittest; and it may be centuries still before the dull and unthinking masses cease to regard hoarding as the highest and chiefest of pursuits. But now, since we know the secret of making gold grow in the recesses of rocks, as mosses grow on the outside, they will no longer hoard gold. And that is the death-blow to the miser and the money-lender.

"You know, when gold was first found in California, English bankers sent commissions to America, urging that silver only be made the commercial basis. So you see that we have only to find gold in such masses as we have silver, a thing still possible, even in the mountains of Russia or the Americas, to destroy it as a basis of trade. And ah what a triumph, what a day of emancipation when we shall proclaim our discovery to the world, and Russia shall let loose her millions from the mines in the Ural; when the bravest and best men of our own great land shall cease to destroy rivers and forests and come out from the Rocky Mountain caverns to the sun and the plains and —"

"And commerce shall cease?"

"Commerce, in its best estate will begin."

"And your currency?"

"Will be honor; as it is now, in nine cases out of ten, nine dollars in ten. A merchant of long standing and stainless name only gives his name, his check, in payment. Is a nation less than a man?

"I tell you that commerce, free and open interchange between men and nations, will only begin when honor is made a basis, instead of base metal,— when this mighty nation of United States shall say to the nations of the earth, as it said to its own people in the late great war, Here is my honor, my promise to pay; I have done with shifting and varying values that wreck and impoverish and make miserable my people —"

"But if—?"

"There should be no such words. We have only to insist on it, to persist in it, and how eagerly other nations will follow! and then the poet's dream, 'the federation of the world!'"

XVIII. — GIVE US THIS DAY OUR DAILY BREAD.

The Day sat by with banner furled;
   His battered shield hung on the wall;
One great star walked the upper world,
   All purple-robed, in Stately Hall;
Some unseen reapers gathered golden sheaves,
The skies were as the tree of life in yellow leaves.

God's poor of Hebron rested. Then
   Straightway unto their presence drew
A captain with his band of men
   And smote His poor, and well-nigh slew,
Saying, "Hence, ye poor! Behold, the king this night
Comes forth with torch and dance and loud delight."

His poor, how much they cared to see!
   How begged they, prone, to see, to hear!
But spake the captain angrily,
   And drove them forth with sword and spear,
And shut the gate; and when the king passed through,
These lonely poor — they knew not what to do.

Lo, then a soft-voiced stranger said:
   "Come ye with me a little space.
I know where torches gold and red
   Gleam down a peaceful, ample place;
Where song and perfume fill the restful air,
And men speak scarce at all. The King is there."

They passed; they sat a grass-set hill —
   What king hath carpets like to this?
What king hath music like the trill
   Of crickets 'mid these silences —
These perfumed silences, that rest upon
The soul like sunlight on a hill at dawn?

Behold what blessings in the air!
  What benedictions in the dew!
These olives lift their arms in prayer;
  They turn their leaves, God reads them through;
Yon lilies where the falling water sings
Are fairer-robed than choristers of kings.

Lift now your heads! yon golden bars
  That build the porch of heaven, seas
Of silver-sailing golden stars —
  Yea, these are yours, and all of these!
For yonder king hath never yet been told
Of silver seas that sail these ships of gold.

They turned, they raised their heads on high;
  They saw, the first time saw and knew,
The awful glories of the sky,
  The benedictions of the dew;
And from that day His poor were richer far
Than all such kings as keep where follies are.

THE stranger, having turned aside from the meditative priest, felt himself drifting again into Miriam's presence. The sun had gone down; the stars were out, and yet it was not night, or at least, it was not dark. Light, light everywhere! Not jets of light, like gas, or electric lights, but level sheets of light, soft, large, and luminous as the face of the moon. But more of this hereafter.

"You will dine with us now?"

He wanted to say that he would like to sit and hear her and her only forever and forever; for that had been the truth. He could not have dared to lie to her, even in compliment; but he assented in silence, and she led on through the luminous woods and walls of glass. They finally entered what seemed to be a grove, with a great table reaching far down and out of sight under broad-sweeping leaves.

He sat at her right hand. Grave and learned men, beautiful and silent women, brown and black and pearly white, were here and there between the men, like fruit among the foliage overhead.

He could see the stars and the moon in the blue sky through the leaves.

"What will you do if it rains?"

With a finger partly raised to her lips, for the music and dancing were about to begin, she said kindly, as she leaned her face so close to his that he breathed the perfume of her hair:—

"The sky which you see is seen through a sky of glass."

The musicians, some distance back and up in the boughs, like singing birds, were not of the old and tired type, bald and exhausted from bad air and bad lights, and broken by care and anxiety; they were ruddy and merry and full of the music of their own high spirits,—girls here, boys there, middle-aged men and middle-aged women; yet all young, young with the eternal youth of love and content and kindliness.

A note! a bar! a breath of warm wind in the trees! Zephyrs? birds? Eolian harps? a far-off call of cooling waters? What was it, and what did it all mean?

Can you conceive of silent music? Well, this was silent music. At least it was music without noise. We need say no more now, we might be misunderstood were we to say less. It was music without the noise that so insolently attends ordinary music. May we say it was noiseless melody?

It was not the music of the civilized city, it was the new music of the new order that is to come, — the wild, free, far-off, and effortless melody of the desert and of the silent children of the desert; of love, peace, pleasure, rest. Suddenly, on a glass stage to the right and left and among the great banana-leaves and lofty ferns with fronded palms that pushed against the sky of glass in heaven, the dancers glided. And they too were noiseless, and they glided as if in the air. The glass was so perfect that, like the artificial sky overhead, it was invisible.

To and fro, forward, back, bowed or erect, singly or in couples, they sang and sang in the movements of their most perfect bodies. The leaves and ferns were very abundant and very broad, and these dancing girls were natural.

Then slowly all sound, all movement of all things ceased. Slowly and unobtrusively a white-haired man, far down among the trees, rose up and solemnly bowed his head. Then all heads were bowed with his; each one present repeated the Lord's Prayer, and that was all.

As he took his seat, a beautiful woman arose and slowly proceeded to read the Sermon on the Mount.

Meantime the dinner went on as if no stranger were present. In fact, the stranger was not allowed to feel that he was a stranger.

And such a dinner! — such milk and honey, such fruit, such oils! Surely the wearied man had come at last upon the land of milk and honey. The Lord had surely led him through the green pastures by the still waters.

And what a continual melody of melodies, even after the girls had melted away one by one from among the ferns and banana-leaves, and the musicians and all had settled into place at table! — a sort of melodious silence! No rattling of knives on rattling plates, in the carving and handling and mutilation of meats, for of meats there were none; no coming and going of servants; no rattling and rasping of feet on marble floors; they sat with their feet on the soft, white, natural sands of the desert.

But this one dining-hall, or temple to melody, was only an example of a constantly increasing number of a similar and yet very dissimilar character; for while the people had their individual homes, they loved to come often to these pleasant dining clubs or halls.

The dining-hall which was devoted to serious themes, and was preferred by venerable men and women of earnest thought, was a smaller and less pretentious place. Yet even here, peace, repose, the perfect good-manners, a low voice, an equanimity of soul and serenity of all things, all things keeping harmonious melody with lisping leaves overhead and soft, warm sands underfoot.

The hall where the men and women who were entirely devoted to science loved to meet and dine was also peculiar to itself, as were those of poetry and painting. But each and all had this dominating preference for nature's harmony of color, harmony of sense, harmony of soul.

And now let us mention one thing here before it is quite forgotten. He had been here many days, had sat at many dinners; yet one day, when passing with his good clergyman through a herd of fat cattle, he suddenly remembered that he had not tasted roast beef since coming to the place.

"You have not tasted roast beef nor any other kind of meat. Olive-oil, butter, eggs, cream, and so on have been your closest approach to meat eating," said the good man, smiling.

"And you do not eat animal food?"

"We do not want animal food here, and we do not need animal food here; and so, of course, we do not eat our sleek and mild-eyed companions."

"Of what use, then, are your herds?"

"For milk, butter, cheese; besides that, when these cattle grow so old that they are helpless, they are driven to a remote place and relieved of life by a painless death; then we permit ourselves to use their hides."

"Yes, you must have shoes."

"Not at all necessary, not at all. Did ever man see such pretty feet as Indian women have? There have never been seen on earth such small and pretty feet as the American Indian women have always had. And yet they, even in the North, are and have always been, so far as possible, a bare-footed people. And here it is not only possible for our women as well as men to go barefooted, but it is even desirable for comfort. No, we do not really need much leather here," added he. " Now, when I work in the field—"

In his surprise at the idea of the Established Church working in the fields the stranger must have suddenly turned his head; for he looked at him inquiringly for a second and then continued:—

"As I was going on to say, when I work in the fields I always go barefooted, for I like the touch of the soft soil and the warm sand. It makes my blood run like wine, and I live in my feet as well as in my head at such a time. My wife, however, still wears shoes when she does her weaving or spinning."

"Your wife? weaving? Pardon me, you are jesting."

" Nay, you shall see her at her weaving some day, and soon. With us the abolition of all special privileges has made it necessary for all to toil. But when all men toil, no man need work hard or beyond his strength. Work, in fact, has become a recreation, a necessity of perfect enjoyment."

"But even when all toil, work must be a hardship."

"Not at all. Two hours a day at any employment will support one nicely."

"But do the rich work also? What pressure brings them to toil?"

"There are no rich in the sense in which you use the word. Of course some men care more for wealth than others, but as they must earn it they must work for it. The State does not equalize possessions, but it equalizes opportunities; and there are no wide differences in possessions such as the outside world shows. Ponder well on this, my son. Inequalities in condition are born out of special favors granted by the State to a few. There are two ways to cure this evil: Extend the same favors to all, or withhold them from the few. We believe in the latter method, which is more truly in harmony with the Declaration of Independence. With us, possession is dependent upon personal toil or the free gift of friendship."

The man pondered. "It is wonderfully simple, but it does not get back of natural differences."

"We do not propose to question nature,"

said the priest, with a lofty look on his face. "The powers of the human brain are infinitely varied. The dullard in one direction may be wondrously skilful in another. Men differ from each other very little more than birds of the same species. Equality of chance will prove this. Freedom is the magic word, and has been through all ages. We are nearing the fulfilment of its prophecy."

The man now spoke hesitatingly; he had another question to ask: —

"But are there not unpleasant tasks which all shirk? Is not some force necessary?"

"I see the question," said the priest. "There is no force in our colony to control the action of the individual, save only when the action interferes with the equal freedom of the rest. We have no slaves on whom to throw our menial tasks. All menial service has disappeared."

"But there must be unpleasant tasks," persisted the man.

"There were at first; but as all were free to do them or not, the most unpleasant soon commanded the highest wages, and the employers were forced to abolish them altogether or make them pleasant. It was marvellous how soon invention turned itself in the direction of making heavy tasks light, and changing or abolishing whole industries. 'Any industry which depends upon the slavery of a single one of my people,' said our great leader, 'will be abolished, because all my people must be free.' This law of freedom has made every mine light as day, every factory silent and sunny, and every menial task a source of forward movement, freedom to freemen."

The good priest's face glowed as he spoke. His smile had tender sympathy in it.

The man caught at the priest's cloak as he rose. "Tell me more!" he cried. "The light is breaking for me."

"Go see for yourself," smiled the priest. You will not find one noisome workshop, not one dark and damp mine, nor one furnace-like place of toil in the city. There will be a lack of many things which have been considered necessary to civilization; but we say that any industry or enterprise which is based upon the enforced toil of our fellow-men is not civilization; it is the infamy of civilization. Come with me. You will not find a toil-worn face, nor a gnarled and trembling, work-scarred hand in this city of ours. Every man, woman, and child in this colony can throw the head back and laugh with joy of life and an unclouded future. Come — to see is to be convinced."

The bewildered man rose and followed the priest. "It is like the law of gravity," he muttered. "It reaches everywhere, this law of equal freedom."

"I'll be patient with you," said the priest. "It troubled me also. No one but Miriam comprehended it at first."

XIX. — THE TOIL OF GOD.

Behold the silvered mists that rise
   From all-night toiling in the corn.
The mists have duties up the skies,
   The skies have duties with the morn;
While all the world is full of earnest care
To make the fair world still more wondrous fair,

More lordly fair; the stately morn
   Moves down the walk of golden wheat;
Her guards of honor gild the corn
   In golden pathway for her feet;
The purpled hills she crowns in crowns of gold,
And God walks with us as He walked of old.

Ah, the mother's love here! the lover's love here! the love in the hearts of all here! the God in the hearts of all!

Our unfortunate city-builder, who had wrought so hard on his mountain-side by the sea and yet had failed so signally, sought out, at every opportunity, the silent and wonderful woman who had done all this since they parted in Egypt. He wanted to sit at her feet and learn. How helpless he was, he now began to know too well. Would she only teach him, tell him how to go on!

They sat one day by the fountain in the Toltec ruins. The birds were busy, the bees were busy.

"Yes, it is all just like that here," she said at length. "We all work together and bring our sweets to the common hive, — not because of law, but because of freedom and plenty."

He bowed his head in meditation for a time, then said: —

"You have succeeded, I have failed. It is but right that you tell me why it is that I, the strong man, should have failed, while you, the woman, and not so strong in body, succeeded. You will tell me?"

After some hesitation she began and went on slowly; for she was very far from strong:

"In the first place you failed by tempting men to leave you and turn back to the taskmasters and the flesh-pots of Egypt. Why, had Moses himself set his children down on a mountain-side in sight of some beautiful city, and offered them the choice to stay or go, how many would have remained with him and gone forward with him to build Jerusalem? William the Conqueror burned his ships behind him, and so kept his sixty thousand at his side. Even the Pilgrim Fathers would have returned, could they have consistently done so, as William Penn returned."

There was a long silence. The bees and

the birds, and the grasshoppers that sung in the grass at their feet had it all their own way. Then she went on: —

"No, we here, removed from almost every temptation, do not allow ourselves nearly the liberty to come and go and evade the first great law of God that you allowed to the lowest of the low, the weakest of the weak, and in the midst of every temptation."

"And that first great law of God is — ?"

"In the sweat of thy face shalt thou eat bread till thou returnest to the ground."

He caught in his breath and said, "Why, I thought the first great law of God was the love of God and to 'love thy neighbor as thyself.'"

"Hear me, hear me," she said. "The very first, last words of God to man, as the gates of Paradise closed behind, were these: 'In the sweat of *thy* face — not in the sweat of the face of another — thou shalt eat bread till thou returnest to the ground;' and we search the Bible in vain for any single exception in favor of any human being, be he priest, prophet, president, or king. Why, even the emperor of the heathen Mongol must plough and sow his field in the sweat of his face. And so firmly fixed is this law of God, established in the laws of nature, that the experience of six thousand years testifies that this is the only path to perfect health. This is a positive law, the first law, and a positive law that admits of no equivocation. It fell from the voice of God centuries before Moses reached up his hands to receive the tablets where His finger, amid thunder and flame, had traced the negative laws of the Decalogue."

"The negative laws?"

"As I said before, this one first law, that thou shalt eat thy bread in the sweat of thy face, is a positive law. The Decalogue is almost entirely negative. But only let the one first great command be strictly observed and the Decalogue will never be broken. It is the one continual effort to escape this one first command that brings man in collision with the laws of Sinai. As for the law of love, it is as natural as nature; though the true reading is not as you read it. After the love of God, which is inseparable from all goodness, you are commanded to 'love thy neighbor *as* thyself.' Do you understand?"

"Certainly, and so I have tried and tried to do."

"But have you not tried to love him more? Mark you, you are to 'love thy neighbor *as* thyself;' not more than thyself, but *as* thyself. Now as you love the good that is in you, so shall you love the good that is in your neighbor; as you hate the evil that is in you, so shall you hate and abhor the evil that is in your neighbor, — yea, hate it and abhor it."

A long time he held his head low in thought now, and she sat listening to the birds, bees, grasshoppers, God. Then he said: —

"Why may not any resolute souls, if wise enough and strong enough, step out from the world and into this unpeopled middle land, anywhere, anywhere from here up to Canada, or even down to Patagonia, and do much as you have done here, with this example of yours before them?"

"It should be done and it will be done, over and over again. The mistake has been in man's not believing in man. Man has said man is bad; kings, politicians, creedists, have kept man arrayed against man since the dawn of history. To-day Europe keeps millions and millions of men standing with guns and swords in hand to slay their brothers — Christians! But this nation has grown beyond that; and now the people of this city have grown beyond the idle lawyers, idle politicians, and idle creedists who continually tell us that man is bad, evil, weak, worthless, and cannot be trusted to go forth from slavery, as Moses went forth, and found his own city in the wilderness."

"Then I shall abandon my mountain-side above the city, and lead my people as Moses led his people, and build my city in the wilderness as you have built yours."

He was very much in earnest, but she raised her thin hand in protest as she said: —

"No; 'what man putteth his hand to the plough and looketh back?' Go forward to the end as you began. An example of great effort, even a great failure, is worth much to the world now. The foundations of cities planted by man in mud and malaria are shaken. Take New York, for example, once a small city of great men, now a great city of small men, who contend and strive and struggle; a city continually divided against itself. And so we know that it shall one day have no place on the map of the world. No, not wars nor earthquakes, nothing of that sort as of old when walls were built, but that lowest of all low pursuits and the coarsest of all human qualities, commerce, money-getting, — this is in her heart to her ruin; this is the baneful wooden horse holding destruction within."

"Yes, yes. And what a miracle has been wrought here!"

"It is not a miracle," she hastened to say; "I simply removed all friction. As for that stupendous work which is being done," and she lifted her face toward the glittering sea of spires and towers beyond, "it has cost scarcely a thought; and it has cost no man any waste of time. The eminent humanitarians who gathered about me here had time, as never before in the history of man, to really think and really be humanitarians. There was an old mercenary saying that time is money. We esteem the man who saves time to man as the only real millionnaire. He is not only a millionnaire, he is the emancipator of the human race."

"Yet Ruskin has said that man should first set man to work, then the cattle, then the machine."

"Yes, and Morris is teaching that we should turn back to the old pastoral times, and live as the shepherds lived." She said this with a sad shake of the head. "Why, this," she went on, "is like as if the two great captains of Moses had turned back to the flesh-pots of Egypt. But at the same time these teachings show us that the world is ripe, ready for open revolt against the hard and bitter conditions of its people."

She paused, and he took the occasion offered to look her in the face, and with bitter remembrances ask her again why he had failed so sadly; why his long endeavor to build up a city on the mountain-side should have been so despised; for he felt she had not told all.

At last she said slowly, sadly, "Why, then, in the second place you failed because of your vanity, your painful and most pitiful vanity."

The sudden flush of pain that swept over his face as his eyes fell before her told how truly the probe had gone to the heart, and how necessary was the cruel surgery. After a pause, and leaning forward her face, she said in the kindest and most pitying manner:

"Your vanity made you choose a conspicuous place, where you could daily proclaim from your housetop how good and humble and industrious and unselfish you were. You thrust yourself and your new ideas in the midst of hard men who had but the one old idea of getting and getting; and then you proclaimed by word and deed that if a man smote the one cheek you would cheerfully turn the other, and that if a man took from you one garment you would not only give another but the whole suit; and so, right in the face of the Lord's Prayer, you led men into temptation."

The weight of her truth bowed his head low before her once more; for he saw that he had, after all, been but a boastful Pharisee. Finally, she went on:—

"The world is dotted all over with good men who are trying to do good in secret; but he who proclaims it,—'verily he *hath* his reward.' Yet go forward. You have not failed; you only have not yet succeeded."

Then from far away, as if from that other world, came her words, His words: "Be ye wise as serpents, but as harmless as doves. . . . I leave my peace with you."

XX.—WHEN MAN IS NOT WATCHING MAN.

I think the bees, the blessed bees,
   Are better, wiser far than we.
The very wild birds in the trees
   Are wiser far, it seems to me;
For love and light and sun and air
Are theirs, and not a bit of care.

What bird makes claim to all God's trees?
   What bee makes claim to all God's flowers?
Behold their perfect harmonies,
   Their common board, the common hours!
Say, why should man be less than these,
The happy birds, the hoarding bees?

The birds? What bird hath envied bird
   That he sings on as God hath willed?
Yet man — what song of man is heard
   But he is stoned, or cursed, or killed?
Thank God, sweet singers of the air,
No sparrow falls without His care.

O brown bee in your honey house?
   Could we like you but find it best
To common build, on sweets carouse,
   To common toil, to common rest,
To common share our sweets with men —
We surely would be better then.

THREE other things I constantly wonder at here," was his remark to her one morning: "The marvellous growth of your groves;

the law and order; and the large intelligence of your people."

"In the first place, to answer you in order, we have here three hundred and sixty-five days in the year, in which to toil, fashion, build. Besides that, these trees, plants, cereals, and all things that spring from the earth, have twelve full and fervid months in which to grow, while in most places they have but four, six, or seven at the farthest. So you see that we have three or four times as many days and months in the year here as in many places. All that this desert, so-called, was waiting for came when we brought the rain and led the water down from the trout streams or up from our artesian wells. The water followed these channels and furrows down through the dust and mud, the dust was watered, the mud was drained, all by means of this same force, and in this same furrow we planted the banana-slip, the olive-branch, the mulberry-tree, and all other sorts of trees from all lands. Then we had only to widen and duplicate the furrows, and sow them with rice, then dam the furrow, and it was flooded and brought to perfection without further effort. Cane, wheat, maize, all things under the sun in fact, came to us and nourished us almost without a stroke or bit of help from our hands. And now here is one thing I must beg you to note distinctly. We not only have had all the time that God has given us because of a kindly clime, but we have husbanded it. We have cherished and housed and husbanded time as others do gold."

He looked into her face inquiringly.

"I will explain," she said. "Civilized man, so-called, spends his time in watching his fellow-man. How many men in eleven are really at work? One! Yes, in the greatest city of earth, London, it takes ten men to watch and keep that one man at work. In the country the proportion of workers and watchers is about evenly divided. Sometimes these English take it into their heads to hang one of their number. They actually spend a lifetime, or what would fully aggregate a long lifetime, in taking that one man's life. But we have no bankers, no landlords, no brokers, no soldiers, no jailers, no idlers indeed of any sort set to watch ourselves. So you see we have to ourselves all the time that God and a genial clime can give. And this answers, in some sort, at least, your first inquiry.

"As for the second, our law and order, we found that here, here with the savages, so-called. It is true they had only the germ; we have given the germ growth. They had laid the keel of our ship of State: we have helped to launch it, that is all. You see the Indian is and always was," she went on, "the truest and most perfect communist. All the lands, horses, products of the fields and chase, everything but the bow in his hand, was as much the property of his brother as himself. And so there was no stealing; there was no temptation to robbery or murder for money or property. With this millstone of temptation taken from about a man's neck, see how tall and erect he would stand! Take away the temptation to lie from the clerk who sells goods, from the grocery-man, the politician, all people, in fact, who live in idleness upon the toil of others, and see what a long and a strong step forward man has made, and how little friction will then be found in the machine of law and order. We have conserved all that was good in the Indian's life, and discarded that which was outgrown. We have continued the common ownership of nature's storehouse, and left to the individual the fruit of his own toil.

"And now as to the third object of your wonder," she said. "We had, as you well know, long contemplated a colony in Palestine, but we finally saw that this would be only a garden for the thistles, and when the crisis came we were quite ready.

"I had at hand the material for the new order of things, so far as brave hearts and ready hands could make it. All we had to do was to transfer ourselves to the spot where we were to set up our tabernacle of pure worship, like the Pilgrim Fathers. True, we were not nearly so numerous then as now, but all the time our friends have been coming; and now, of course, since all things flourish so wonderfully, they will come in astonishing numbers. And they will be, as they have been from the first, of the very best, — men and women who believe in man and his glorious destiny; men and women who care for man, and are content to let God take care of Himself; men and women who dare not presume to speak for God, but keep silent and let Him speak for Himself; men and women who devoutly adore all that is good and beautiful, — lovers, believers; men and women who here have time to meditate and see more clearly; men and women who with that dignity of soul which is the only true humility, and that humility of soul which is the only true dignity, begin to see, and to say lovingly, one to another, ' The infinite God is " the aggregate man." ' "

XXI.

> Man's books are but man's alphabet;
> Beyond and on his lessons lie —
> The lessons of the violet,
> The large, gold letters of the sky.

ONE day, in his quiet rounds through this new Eden on earth, and when quite alone, he came upon a group of gray-haired and serene men and women of most venerable aspect. They were gathered in a grove by a fountain near a field of corn. Not far away were herds of cattle ruminating on the sloping brown hills. Farther on and still up toward the higher land were flocks of sheep, white and restful as summer clouds.

As he approached this quiet group of venerable people, they, rather by act than word, made him one of their number, and he sat down in silence on a little hillock of wild grass in the shadow of a broad palm-tree.

How perfectly serene, how entirely satisfied they all seemed! how unlike the garrulous and nervous and never-satisfied old women of the social world in the great cities in which he had dwelt, were these tranquil and serene old women here! They were beautiful women, beautiful in body as in soul. They literally made man in love with old age, even before they had opened their lips to speak in their low, sweet fashion.

And these benign and restful men! He began to recall the old men, old beaux, roués, whom he encountered in London, Paris, Rome, — their wrinkles, powder, paint; their terror at the approaches of time; their dismay at the thought of death; their lies, lies on their lips, lies in every act of their lives, their lustful lies to women, — their whole foul and most despicable existence.

"Ah me!" thought he, "why may a man not grow in grandeur as he grows in years, like the mighty trees of the forest? Is a man less than a tree? Shall a man who is made in God's image make himself less than a tree?"

"We meet here, or in some other like pleasant place, daily," began one of the most venerable men, "to take lessons. We are children at school, you see;" and he smiled pleasantly on the group of gray heads under the palms round about.

"But you have no books."

"We desire thought rather than books. If Shakespeare found in the books of his day only 'words, words, words,' what shall be said of the books now that deluge the earth?"

"But we have books every now and then that gleam like lightning through a cloud."

"Yes, there are veins of gold in almost every mountain, glints of light in almost every storm-cloud, as you suggest; but why have the storm at all? Why labor with the mountain of old errors or take light from the cloud, when the world is all light if we will but see the light?"

"And books will not help you to see the light?"

"Hold a book up before your face continually, and how much of the sun can you see?" asked the old man, earnestly. "No, the world has run all to words, as a luxuriant garden runs to weeds in the autumn; the press, the pulpit — all words, words, words!" said the old man finally.

The stranger could but recall the protest of Christ, as the kindly old man concluded and was silent. He remembered that enduring truths have been born in the desolate places; that the Ten Commandments came down to us out of the most savage mountain ever seen; that Christ grew to manhood in the woods of Nazareth; that the

Koran was written on storm-bleached bones in a cave; that the face of God was seen in the desert only of old, and that it was only to a houseless boy on the plains of Shinar, where he found a stone for a pillow, that the ladder of heaven was let down.

"The one main duty of man to man is to convince him that death is a thing not to be feared, but, in its ordinary course, to be desired above all things," said the master of the quiet little school; and he continued: "To convince him of this he must be convinced of his immortality. He must not only be convinced of his immortality, but he must be convinced that he begins life in the next world precisely where he attains to in this; that in this way, and this way only, is it possible for a man to really lay up treasures in heaven. And to convince a man of his immortality and of the preservation of his treasures in heaven is to develop the best that is in him and all that is in him. In order that all his senses may be developed, he must return to nature and nature's God. Why should the silly sheep have sense of sight, smell, taste, superior to our own? Why should even a dog be able to look a man in the face, or smell his footprints, and know more about him in a minute than a man may learn in a year? Not long ago, while spending the night among the cattle, so that I might learn from them, I saw some rise up and move aside and look, as if they saw God or angels pass; or as if Christ had come again to companion with the beasts of the stalls."

The master was silent a time; then, as none of his companions spoke, but all seemed inclined to listen further, he went on:

"Thousands of years ago, we know man met God and the angels face to face; but in grasping after gains, going out to battle, cultivating only the sense of acquisition and of destruction, man has fallen even behind the brute in the finer senses of vision and apprehension of the beautiful and good. But here, at last, after all the ages of blackness and brutality, man finds place and time to sit down and meditate in silence and soberness, and to live by the precepts of the Sermon on the Mount."

He again rested, and waited for the words of others. As no one spoke, the master said to them:—

"You do well to meet daily, to meditate continually; for never had man such responsibility; because never had man, since that other Eden, such opportunity. You do well to leave behind you all books, the dreary history of continuous crimes and bloodshed on the one hand, and the weary round of lengthened prayers for impossible things on the other hand. You have a right to be happy, continually happy, as you are here. Nay, more; I assert that it is not only your right to be happy, but it is your duty to be happy; and beyond this lies the boundless duty to the world. Let us follow the footprints of Christ, so that we may in some fair day overtake Christ, and then will the sad and weary world follow in our footprints and be glad and be good. Let us cultivate our senses by pure and peaceful and unselfish lives, till we at length have the discernment of dumb brutes. Let us teach the world that if it will only lift up its face from money-getting on earth it may see God in heaven."

XXII. — THE TRULY BRAVE.

And what for the man who went forth for the right,
Was hit in the battle and shorn of a limb?
Why, honor for him who falls in the fight,
Falls wounded of limb and crippled for life;
Give honor, give glory, give pensions for him,
Give bread and give shelter for babes and for wife.

But what for the hero who battles alone
In battles of thought where God set him down;
Who fought all alone and who fell overthrown
In his reason at last from the hardness and hate?
Why, jibe him and jeer him and point as you frown
To that lowly, lone hero who dared challenge fate.

God pity, God pardon, and God help us all!
"That young man of promise," wherever he be,
"That young man of promise," wherever he fall, —
For fall, he must fall, 't is a thousand to one, —
Let us plant him a rose; let us plant a great tree
To hide his poor grave from the world and the sun.

I tell you 't were better to cherish that soul —
That soldier that battles with thought for a sword,
That climbs the steep ramparts where wrong has control,
And falls beaten back by the rude, trampling horde.
Ay, better to cherish his words and his worth
Than all the Napoleons that people the earth.

"I AM going to the hospital before breakfast to-morrow; it lies some forty miles out in the mountains. We go by electric train. Will you go?"

"Gladly."

"But ah," and here she was sad and thoughtful, "this is a sad case I am going out to look after. The woman is a friend of mine, a princess by birth, and when in the world, the struggling world, as you know it, she was always very ambitious of distinction. Thinking herself cured of that, or rather hoping to become quite cured of it here, she came to me only a year ago. But alas! In less than a year after her arrival she grew again ambitious, and, desiring a high place as director, she grew so desperate as to tell a falsehood to some others, who, like herself, had newly come and had not yet grown strong."

"And she was detected?"

"Oh, no, not detected; not nearly so bad as that. She came and told me the next day; and she then went and told all to whom she had talked; and when the court sat in judgment she stood up and made public confession. Then she condemned herself to the hospital for half a year. I begged the judge that she should not be permitted to sentence herself so severely; but the judge thought the punishment none too hard, and so let her go to the hospital the full time for which she had sentenced herself."

"For which she had sentenced herself?"

"Yes. You see our hospital here for mental maladies and physical ailments is the same. We try to be even more gentle with those who have maladies of the mind than those who have ailments of the body; for a man may lose a limb and yet, if his mind is clear, he does not suffer nearly so much as one with an afflicted mind. Besides, a mental ailment, rare with us, fortunately, is much more subtle and hard to master than a physical one. Take this case for example. For generations back, her family, a most noble Polish one, had been bitterly impoverished; and you can easily see how with their pride and poverty together they transmitted their misery to this poor friend of mine who is now serving out her time in the hospital."

He found the "hospital" a sort of summer watering place; not a Newport or a Saratoga, however. It was a Christian place, not noisy in the least nor devoted to any sort of folly to attract attention. All the invalids, mental or physical, from down in the valley were here. The new mothers were in a similar retreat further on. He found many people coming and going, these fragrant pine groves being cooler and the air more invigorating than in the great valley below. All the mental sick, "convicts" we call them in Christian lands, kept themselves at some sort of work in attending on the physical sick. And yet the numerous visitors kept heaping attention on the "convicts;" more attention, indeed, did they receive than those who had only bodily ailments.

He was so enchanted with the humanity, the heart, the real Christianity in all he saw here, that his whole soul was filled with exultation at the possibilities of the future.

"You will have a city here, such a city, in magnitude and glory, as the world has never seen," he said, as they walked the hospital grounds together.

Pausing for a moment, she raised her head and answered, "It is possible. But cities, great cities, as a rule, should not be." Then she said, after a moment's silence, "True, we must have centres. Each division of the earth, natural or artificial, great or small, must have a common centre, a heart. The hands, the feet, all have their functions and they all have laws of health; but with the means of transportation without cost within the reach of all, great cities will not be built. Population in the outside world is growing denser because of the greed of landlords and the folly of granting railway privileges, which makes transportation difficult. With our rapid free transit, our railways supported out of the rental value of our land, we keep our city like a garden, as you see. No, I would sweep great cities, like New York and London, from the face of the earth. We know that sword and flood and flame have been against cities from the first dawn of history. Pestilence, the very hand of God, has ever been turned against all great cities. Children die in cities, men and women are dwarfed in cities. No great man has ever yet been born in a great city. A city is a sin and a shame, a crime against the human race. Each man must have his acre, his vine and figtree, his place of retreat, his grove, his temple, his shrine where he may pray, may meditate, may be all himself."

In the cool of the evening they took the cars for the city.

"As time goes by," said the good angel on their descent to the city, "we shall have much less mental sickness. Take for example this poor friend of mine, who, happily, is now about to be restored to us entirely healed. Had she, and her ancestors as well, been born and reared in these restful ways, no such sickness would ever have overtaken her. As for bodily sickness, that is partly our own fault; but death, all know, is not to be avoided and should not be undesired. Yet I surely think that mental sickness can be swept from the earth. You remember the poor nude idiots who used to swim out to us every few days as we sailed up the Nile? They call these poor creatures God's people there, you remember, and the boatmen feed them and care for them as best they can. We, that is, civilized Europe and America, lock them up! Out here we hope to go back to first causes and help nature to make the crooked straight.

"And bodily illness," she continued, "is not to be wondered at when we consider what man has done, and is still doing in most of the world, to destroy himself. Look at France! Russia! Sixteen hours of toil in all sorts of weather, and such food! food that is scarcely fit for wild beasts. Still man must have exercise if he would have a healthy body. I observed, when in prison with my poor father, that all who were confined esteemed a few hours of exercise in the open air above their bread. Every man, as a rule, who is shut up in prison, spends from four to ten hours daily in pacing up and down. So it became clear to me that man's body demanded at least six hours of exercise. Less than this would be fatal to his health. A great excess of this would weary him, tax him too heavily, and so leave a loophole by which disease might enter. Now we find here that two hours of work in the fields and gardens by each man will more than feed his family. This amazes you, I know."

"He may work twenty-four hours in a week, twenty-four days of a European laborer's work in a whole year and have all the rest of the year for study, for art, for development?" asked the man.

"If he does that work daily, yes. But we allow no taskmasters here; all is voluntary. After each day of public work a man goes back to his house, among his bees, birds, roses, vines, with his children, and all the other delightful things that go to refresh mind and body and make interesting the spot he has set apart as his home."

Shortly after this delightful day, as the weather grew warmer in the city, they once more visited the pleasant and refreshing pines on the mountain-side. And here they walked and they talked as before.

"Would you care to walk a little further on among the pines?"

She said this seriously, looking in his face in a quiet and inquiring way, and for answer he moved on at her side in silence.

Half an hour, up the hill and over the hill, through the tall, open pines, and he saw before them, in a wooded depression of the landscape through which a little mountain stream wound in the long, strong grass, a few scattering graves where roses grew in careless profusion. Some deer were feeding on the slope of the hill a little beyond, and beyond these, higher on the sloping hill where the pines stood dark and dense, he saw what at first seemed to be several large, old-fashioned marble tombs.

"No, they are not tombs," she said softly. "These are simply heaps of sweet-smelling pine wood kept ready for men and women of advanced thought whom we have among us."

"Funeral pyres?"

"Even so. You will understand that here with us in this new order of things there is nothing arbitrary. Minds have different degrees of development. Some have ascended high, some higher still; while many of us still stand at the bottom of the hill and see the plain of life only from the dead level of custom. And so each looks at life, and death also, from his or her own standpoint. Some of us still want priests to lean upon; some of us still at times are weak enough to want to worship idols or even the golden calf; and so, equal freedom is accorded all, for out of freedom will come real development, and every secure step upward must be of gradual ascent; because there is danger of the weak growing weary and of faltering by the way or turning back.

"Ah, I see," he said. "Here conspicuously in the front are the graves of those who claim attention even in the tomb."

"That is it," she sadly answered, as she looked about and on up the hill beyond into the deep, dark shadows. But up yonder, in the silence and obscurity, the remains of those who have outgrown such folly, like Charles Dickens, Lord Houghton, and others who begged for simple burial, are laid on the fragrant wood as soon as may be after the breath has left the body, in the same garments, in the garments in which death finds them. A flash, a flame; and they are of the clouds and ashes."

XXIII. — GOING.

What if we all lay dead below;
   Lay as the grass lies, cold and dead
In God's own holy shroud of snow,
   With snow-white stones at foot and head,
With all earth dead and shrouded white
   As clouds that cross the moon at night?

What if that infidel some night
   Could then rise up and see how dead,
How wholly dead and out of sight
   All things with snows sown foot and head
And lost winds wailing up and down
The emptied fields and emptied town?

I think that grand old infidel
   Would rub his hands with fiendish glee,
And say, "I knew it, knew it well!
   I knew that death was destiny;
I ate, I drank, I mocked at God,
Then as the grass was, and the sod."

Ah me, the grasses and the sod,
   They are my preachers. Hear them preach
When they forget the shroud, and God
   Lifts up these blades of grass to teach
The resurrection! Who shall say
What infidel can speak as they?

NEARLY half a year had swept by.

"You are thinking of going away," she said, as they walked together by the great fountain that burst up from the old Toltec ruins near her door; for she was not strong enough to walk further now. It was in the afternoon.

"You knew my thoughts, then?"

"You are going away if — if I go."

"Yes."

"I will go with you." She said this, not sadly, but almost cheerfully, as she leaned heavily on his arm on turning to her door.

There were those here who made one in love with old age; but this woman was making him in love with death.

"You are going back to the work that is before you! I will go with you." And that is all she said about his going or staying; but he felt that it was her desire that he should go.

"I know so many weak and weary people who would be glad to come to this Paradise," he said. "As for myself, I am strong now. I will go back to my work, but shall I not be permitted to send some whom I know, out of the shadow, to this fervid sunlight of yours?"

She raised her hand with effort, and, pointing to some pale weeds that grew in a dark and shaded corner beneath the broad banana-leaves, she bade him, more by sign than word, to pull them from the ground and lay them before her in the sun. He did so, and they laid their drooping heads down on the hot sands and died.

"You see," she said; "and yet our choicest flowers are only cultivated weeds. Pull them up and place them in the sun suddenly, and you do not help them; you simply kill them. It is well to have great examples like this, our City Beautiful, but the world must improve itself slowly, naturally, by force of the example we have set of freedom, truth, and justice. No, we must have strong pillars, like the Pilgrim Fathers, and, God willing, we shall have a temple reared in time that will shelter all. Our example will uplift the world."

She rested for a long time now. Finally she said, "You will go up to the hospital and remain — remain until you see a sign."

He bowed silently in assent; for she was too near the other world for him to question now or make any protest. Then she said : —

"I like those people up there; I like the guilty ones, those whom you call convicts; but we do not call them that. Why, when one of your poor, unfortunate people is accused of crime, the State, the State's attorney, the whole power of the State is exerted, and no pains or money spared to prove that man guilty, — as if it were a good thing for the State to have a guilty man! Ah, how you forget that 'it is better that ten guilty ones escape than that one innocent man should suffer.'"

She was exhausted now and breathed with effort. Yet it seemed as if with her last breath she must teach this most important lesson. After a time she added: —

"What a pity that all the State should array itself against one man, bound in irons, in an iron tomb, as if it were a glorious thing for the State to find one of its people with mind so weak or morals so weak that he fell into the pit of temptation." She was silent a long time, then said: —

"You will go now. Good-by again; good-by!"

He arose and stood before her. He fell on his knees and took her hand. "You feel certain, confident, confident that Christ is the Saviour of the world?" he cried; for he felt that she was surely dying.

Steadily, and with a strange light in her eyes, as if it might be the light of another world, she looked him long and silently in the face. Then she said slowly and in a voice so soft and low: —

"Yes, yes, Jesus Christ is the Saviour of the world; but Jesus Christ died to save man from man, — not to save man from God."

He kissed her hand tenderly in silence, and in tears passed out.

XXIV. — PUT UP THY SWORD.

And who the bravest of the brave;
  The bravest hero ever born?
'T was one who dared a felon's grave,
  Who dared to bear the scorn of scorn.
Nay, more than this; when sword was drawn
  And vengeance waited for His word,
He looked with pitying eyes upon
  The scene, and said, "Put up thy sword."
Oh God! could man be found to-day
As brave to do, as brave to say?

"Put up thy sword into its sheath."
  Put up thy sword, put up thy sword!
By Cedron's brook thus spake beneath
  The olive-trees our valiant Lord,
Spake calm and king-like. Sword and stave
  And torch, and stormy men of death
Made clamor. Yet He spake not, save
  With loving word and patient breath,
The peaceful olive-boughs beneath,
"Put up thy sword within its sheath."

A BASHED that he had remained so long, knowing as he did that this inspired soul was about to enter upon another life, the man hastened to take the first conveyance to the mountains of pine.

"You will remain there till you see a sign." He kept saying this as he went his way speaking to no one. He had been with her. His soul, his whole self, this day at least, must be his own and inviolate. He did not go directly to the hospital, to men, but to the woods, to God.

Some scarlet berries, red with the blood of the dying autumn, wreathed the moss-made tomb of a prone monarch of the mountains, on which he sat. All was silent, so silent, save a far, faint melody that came up the mountain-side through the pines, came fitfully on the wind, as one that is weary and would go home to rest.

The tawny carpet of pine quills grew golden as the sun lay level and in spars and bars and beams about him. The huge and lofty trunks of the mighty pine-trees on the mountains round about took on a hue of gold as the sun fell down. The foliage all about grew red, then gold, then yellow. The carpet of pine quills, reaching miles and miles away on either hand and far up the mountains beyond, became gold, a broken, billowy sea of molten gold. And as he sat there, throned amid this mobile sea of fragrant yellow, of color so perfect that it was not only color but form, form, perfume and melody also, he not only saw this color, he heard it. An hour passed.

Then suddenly, as he thought of her, he saw a form, the yellow form and comely shape of a desert lion standing, waiting, removed from him but by a little space.

And even as he looked, the sinking sun came softly through the forest boughs, a long, slanting shaft of light, and laid a red sword at his feet.

Day had surrendered to night, light to darkness, mortality to immortality.

. . . .

He remained alone all night in the warm woods, but saw no further sign. It was enough.

With the dawn there came up the mountain-side the sweetest, saddest melodies ever known. It was the funeral train.

He took an old man aside. They rested a time beneath the pines. He implored him to tell all, all. "What did she say? What did she do? All, all,—tell me all!" But the old man seemed dazed. He kept silent for some time. At last he spoke.

"I went to her immediately as you left her. I can hardly recall her words. They were words of fire and gold. 'Prove to me, to the world, that man shall surely rise,' I cried. She half turned away her face as in reproach at first, but soon, looking tenderly at me, she said in a low, firm voice, 'Nay, I cannot quite prove to you that man shall rise after death. I cannot quite prove to you that yonder setting sun will rise to-morrow; but I surely, surely believe it will rise;' and then she made a sign that I must leave her to meet God alone. After a little time young musicians came as had been their custom, and played before her door under the palm-trees. And then there came many singers, and they sang, sang as the musicians played, and the sun went down. Then suddenly we heard her voice, like a thread of gold in the woof of harmony, woven in with a most cunning hand. We had never heard her sing before. It was, perhaps, her first as it was her last song.

"There are many birds and of many hues, as you well know, in the foliage of the court there. Well, as the song ceased and the music died away, an old man, older and better than I, and so able to see more of better things than I can see, saw a bird, a wide-winged bird, and white like snow. And after circling above our heads, it flew out through the wide, high trees into the falling night. That was all. We bowed low our heads and wept in pity for ourselves."

Remembering having heard her deplore the sad habit of the world in staring at the wan, worn faces of the helpless dead, he overcame this last desire, as he had overcome others through her teachings and example, and saw her face of clay never more.

And yet he felt, knew, knew positively all the while, that she would come to him, sooner or later, if he only kept his soul refined and fit to see her; and more than that, he knew that she would come to him in her perfection, as she was when she touched the high-tide mark of health and perfection of form and face; for this is in the order of nature. The tide shall touch its topmost limit. The human soul shall not be less than the sea.

Knowing all this, knowing that she would have given back to her all that had been taken away, and that she, and all others who love sincerity, would begin the next life at the high-tide mark in this, and knowing, surely knowing that he should see her thus, how careful was he to say naught, do naught that would make him less worthy to lift his face to hers.

. . . .

They bore her form up, up to her mountain-side, mantled close in the robes in which she died, and none were cruel enough to seek to look into her tired face.

There was a depression in the great heap

of sweet-smelling pine that lay farthest up the hill beyond the hospital, and here they laid the body.

A flame, a long, vapory cloud of smoke tossing to the pine tops, and all turned away. No more cost and no more care, — a little heap of ashes! and around the edges of this little burned spot tall, slim grasses came to stand in circle soon, and shy, wild flowers joined their hands and drooped their heads there tearfully when the rains had come.

. . . .

"So you are going away to-night? Well, the Gulf Stream of the upper seas is reversed at this season. The Japan currents flow towards us in the first few months, but later in the year, as now, Alaska draws on us for heat and things are reversed. You will have quite as pleasant sailing back as when you came."

This was the venerable man who had seen the cattle rise up in the fields at night, as if God was walking by. So fine were his senses that he had only to come into your atmosphere to know your thought. They were walking up the mountain. Without a word the man lifted his eyes. The car of the air-ship swung graceful as a pine cone in the gathering wind at the high platform from which he had descended on coming to the place. They passed up together in silence. What need of words at such a time?

Grasping the old man's hand, he stepped within the car and was about taking his seat when, with a boom as if being propelled by sound, the car bounded away above the clouds and held her course strong and steady toward the north.

He sank into his seat, bowed his head, and moaned, " She said she would be with me!"

After a time he lifted his face, for he felt that he was not alone, and lo! there she sat before him, in all the splendor of youth and strength and divinity of presence. All the majesty of perfect womanhood was with her now. Never, indeed, had he seen her so radiantly, so imperiously beautiful. The same sweet touch of tenderness, the same pathos and pity in the Madonna face, it is true; but over and above this there was a sense of strength and directness and immortality, such as you feel when the sun is rising.

She did not speak; for oh, how futile, lame, harsh, and angular are words! The use of words shall pass away, is passing.

> Why, know you not soul speaks to soul?
> I say the use of words shall pass —
> Words are but fragments of the glass,
> But silence is the perfect whole.

She did not speak but her soul continually said to his soul, " The kingdom of heaven is at hand." And it was said as if in a great court of woods and falling waters, with walls of sapphire, where hung, in letters of fire and gold, the Sermon on the Mount and the Lord's Prayer.

He did not mistake their meaning. He would go forward and these should guide him still. All Israel was forty years in the wilderness, and he had been but five. Surely he should, he could, and he would gather strength and go forward. For she had annihilated the vast space that had been so long between heaven and earth and had brought them almost together — " The kingdom of heaven is at hand."

She did not speak; and yet her soul spoke as certainly in its calm, sweet fashion, wisely, silently; the wisdom of earth in earthly things, the glory, the beauty, the peace of heaven over all.

" I leave my peace with you." " The kingdom of heaven is at hand."

And her soul said to his soul, " Service is

the handmaiden of heaven. Let the Christian run forward with the Sermon on the Mount in hand, swift-footed to meet her. Only see to it that the newly emancipated slave does not fall into a deeper servitude. For man, intoxicated with opportunity, still believes that opulence is happiness. They are fastening again the broken chains, and gathering gold as never was gold gathered before.

"It was the toiler, not the money-changer, who taught the lightnings to talk, created light out of space, and from the airy, white vapors of heaven called into existence the thundering black cavalry of commerce by land and by sea. Take care that this emancipated toiler is not made the slave of his own creations by blind, intoxicated money-changers. See to it that all toil, that none but the helpless live on the toil of others."

Such were the woman's thoughts, words, as they seemed to sail and sail by the porch of heaven above the clouds as before. Then they passed down, down and through the clouds, and it was almost light.

And daring to look full in her face by the coming light he saw a star, then the star only, the bright and beautiful morning star to the east, through the dove-colored leaves of his olive-trees.

And he arose and went to his toil with content and courage and a broad, deep charity in his heart. A dove sang from an olive-tree, the dove and the olive-branch as of old, and the man sang with the dove that day of all days. For had he not seen her? Whether she was of heaven or of earth, who should say? But surely he had been with her entirely, and this was the unuttered song of his heart. He sang silently, for what human voice can approach the plaintive and tender voice of the dove? But here is the song of his heart: —

> Come listen, O love, to the voice of the dove,
>   Come hearken and hear him say,
> " There are many to-morrows, my love, my love,
>   There is only one to-day."
>
> And all day long I can hear him say,
>   " This day in purple is rolled;
> And the baby stars of the Milky Way,
>   They are cradled in cradles of gold."

www.ingramcontent.com/pod-product-compliance
Lightning Source LLC
Chambersburg PA
CBHW020921230426
43666CB00008B/1522